"Jodine's practical and common sense teaching makes it easy for her students to understand exactly what it is they are trying to achieve. It is then no big deal to progress rapidly with their new found knowledge and Jodine makes it fun as well as well as informational."

Jane Holderness Roddam, Olympic Gold Medalist, Author of over 20 books.

"What is important in Jodine's training methods is her consideration, making the journey safe, reasonable and heart centered, holding the well-being of the horse above the agenda of the human."

Liz Mitten Ryan, Co-Author of One With the Herd, The Truth According to Horses, Life Unbridled and Sabbatical.

"Jodine has done a wonderful job of weaving together the many aspects required for effective communication between ourselves and our horses. She has also taught us the importance of understanding, exposing and connecting to our own feelings and emotions as a prerequisite to understanding and connecting to the horse, thus enabling the horse to become the healer. Jodine has successfully delivered her message: Horses are in our lives to teach us partnership, honesty and harmony. Well done...."

Marijke van de Water, B.Sc., DHMS, Equine Health & Nutrition Specialist, Author of "Healing Horses: Their Way!"

IF YOUR HORSE COULD TALK

COULD TALK

Jodine Carruthers

ISBN: 0986894117
ISBN-13: 9780986894114

Harmonious Horsemanship

To my parents, Margaret and Tony, for always loving me, believing in me, and supporting me, unconditionally.

And

In memory of my Gran, Pamela Carruthers, whose dedication and love for horses and the sport of show jumping has touched so many lives, including my own.

Table of Contents

Part 2: Interspecies Communication........33

Acknowledgments

Horses have led me on an incredible journey that would never have been possible without my wonderful family. Words can never express how much gratitude I have for my parents, who have supported me on every step of this journey. Having a daughter who lets horses and intuition lead her life must be terrifying at times. Yet my Mom and Dad have always encouraged me to follow my heart. I also want to thank my sister, Samantha, for putting up with her horse-crazy little sister.

I owe many, many thanks to my grandmother, Pamela Carruthers, for making sure I had horses in my life and inspiring me to want to profoundly influence the horse industry as she did for so many years.

I also want to extend a huge thank you to my husband, Dana Buydens, for bringing so much laughter and joy into my life. His patience and support as I follow my dreams are admirable.

Over the years I have been privileged to have many great teachers and instructors. While there are too many to name, the following people were great influences in my early years: Jane James, Wendy Walker, Gail Pellizzari, Judy Ross, Cheryl Keith, Bridget Flynn, Shiovean Woods, Victor Hugo Vidal, Albert Kley, and Claudia Cojocar. I would also like to express my gratitude to Nick, Kost, and Jenny Karazissis as well as the rest of the "Far West Family" for allowing me to blossom into the rider I am today.

I learned a great deal about horses and life during my time in the Santa Ynez Valley. I wish to thank Monty Roberts, Crawford Hall, and the MRILC Instructors for their dedication to sharing their knowledge of horse psychology and the body language of Equus. I have so much appreciation for the very gifted Castro brothers, Rodolfo, Manuel, and Felipe. They welcomed me into their lives and taught me so much about what it really means to be a horse person. A special thanks to Chris and Hermine for being there for me at the times when I most needed support.

I am grateful to those who started me on my quest for self-exploration and discovery of interspecies communication. They helped me gain clarity on how to move forward on my journey.

I also need to acknowledge all the people who have helped me discover my true purpose. There are so many of you and I am grateful to each one of you. To Deborah Marshall I owe a special thanks for helping me access my horse wisdom and bringing me to a deeper understanding of trauma and self-regulation.

I am so appreciative of Michelle Ross for her guidance and assistance in bringing the breathing exercise and visualization exercises to life. I am also grateful to Amber Coyne for illustrating the "horse in a box" diagram.

I also must mention my business mentor Lisa Arie. This book sparked a desire to share my work with the world, and I feel so fortunate to have found someone who works with me in the way I work with horses. It is truly a gift.

A special thank you to my clients, especially Cheryl, Leigh, and Rhonda. Their dedication to their horses and their willingness to share their stories is inspiring. Thank you to Leigh, Deborah, and Susan for taking the time to read my book and provide valuable feedback.

Finally, these acknowledgments would not be complete without the mention of the many wonderful and amazing horses that have changed my life, again and again. There are far too many to list, but my personal horses must be mentioned: Quantez, Pacific Shadow, Jolly Olly, Apollo, Breeze, Mister, Isabella, and Caesar.

Foreword

Jodine Carruthers has written a truly absorbing and inspirational book about her experiences with horses. She shares with the reader a wonderfully frank and informative series of stories on how she worked with a variety of different horses and ponies, as well as the concepts and methods she used. This is no ordinary narrative on what has come to be called natural horsemanship. It gives the reader a real insight into how important it is to understand and communicate with the horse if we are ever going to be able to build up a true partnership with this amazing animal.

For centuries the horse has been the mainstay of numerous civilizations and has helped man as a beast of burden, a means of transport, a war horse, as food, as a riding and competition horse and as a special companion. To do these tasks much has been demanded of him, and he has willingly performed to the best of his ability. Unfortunately, far too often a lack of knowledge and understanding on the human part has led to domineering and stress inducing practices which result in unpredictable and difficult behaviour from the horse.

The refreshing theme demonstrated throughout this book helps the reader to more fully understand the individuality of our horses and how to learn more about their psychology, means of communication, their body language and their strengths and weaknesses. Horses are non judgemental, but do respond to being treated as equals and individuals. Often what might work with one may not do so with another. The case studies mentioned are fascinating and cover many everyday scenarios that so many of us will have encountered. As a noted Equine Behavior Specialist, Jodine has very successfully depicted how to work with the horse by building a lasting partnership through Harmonious Horsemanship. This should ensure a very special relationship for all who truly want to understand our friend the horse.

Jane Holderness-Roddam
Olympic Gold Medalist

Preface

Wow, what a journey. When I started out writing this book I had no idea that it would end up as it has. The horses have continued to share with me new insights, observations, and understanding on a daily basis. This in turn has caused a consistent evolution in Harmonious Horsemanship, and this book. The deeper the connections I experience with horses, the more I come to realize that we are only beginning to tap into the potential of the horse/human relationship. I am so excited to see where we will be in another ten years.

I chose the title 'If Your Horse Could Talk' while I was sitting around the table with a group of fellow writers, trying to explain my book and the purpose behind it. I said, "It's about all the things horse have taught me over the years. It's all the things that they would share with their owners, riders and handlers if they could talk." And everyone turned to me and said, "That's it!" So the following is a guide book straight from the hearts, and the mouths, of our equine friends.

It has become clear to me that this incredible journey with horses has only been possible because I allow myself to be led by the pure joy that I feel when I am with them. Over the years there have been many times when I have lost touch with that feeling of joy and wondered if my path with horses was over. Yet each time as I closed the chapter on one experience, another chapter began as I found another way to be with horses that once again brought back the joy of the horse/human relationship.

That's not to say the path is always easy or comfortable. Even now as I know how much joy sharing this work with others brings, and I start on a new journey of creating a global company to share this work, I often feel scared and uncomfortable. Taking all the lessons the horses have taught me into the business world is a new experience, and with that come new gifts and new challenges. But the joy I feel when I see a horse and a human experience each other in a whole new way is worth every ounce of fear and discomfort. I know I am safe and I am doing just what I am here to do. Even more importantly I know I am doing it simply for the joy of doing it. Life can't get much better than that.

Introduction

This book has been a long time coming. I am constantly thinking of just one more story or one more idea to add. Throughout my life, horses have been my friends, my family, my partners, and my teachers. More recently, they have become my co-facilitators as I take the gifts they have shared with me to others. Yet no matter where I am or who I am with, horses constantly challenge me to grow and be an even better person. They push me to reach my fullest potential and help others achieve theirs.

I believe that a shift is taking place in our world and in the horse industry. We are moving away from disconnect and dominance and toward communication, authentic leadership, and deeper connection. We have just begun to touch on the depth of relationship we can share with horses and with each other. I believe that horses are finally being heard and that the gifts they have to share with us are priceless. Horses have been trying to share these gifts with us for centuries, but our human egos have been so focused on dominating these incredible animals that we have not given them a chance to share.

This is, of course, a generalization of the horse industry to some degree. I have been involved in many aspects of both the traditional and natural horsemanship industry and met many individuals who defy these generalizations. At the same time, I have met many people who exemplify them, whether they admit it or not. I believe there has actually been too much separation of both the traditional and natural horsemanship industries. When I look at the concepts behind classical training and natural horsemanship methods, there are indeed many similarities. The natural horsemanship trend has just brought many of these concepts to the everyday horse person.

I extend a huge amount of gratitude to the pioneers of the natural horsemanship industry for introducing the general public to horse psychology and body language. But it is time to take horsemanship to the next level. Many natural horsemanship trainers still focus on dominating the animal while talking about gaining trust. Horse psychology and body language are often used to the animal's detriment rather than for his benefit. Often this is not done intentionally, yet it is a by-product of people being taught skills without being taught the concepts behind them. When a person knows a series of moves but has not learned how to read or "feel" the horse's communications, it is still a one-sided partnership. The same is true of the traditional horse industry.

So how do we take horsemanship to the next level? We complete the puzzle. Horse psychology, body language, ground work skills, and riding skills are only a few pieces of the puzzle. Areas such as interspecies communication, the language of energy, self-regulation, and understanding the autonomic nervous system, self-awareness, and recognition of a horse's uniqueness are aspects that need to be explored to fulfill the potential of the horse/human relationship. If we can share our knowledge of the domesticated world with horses and allow them to help us reconnect within ourselves, we will create true win/win partnerships.

There is a balance between teaching horses and learning from them that many of us are ready to explore. For many years I struggled, wondering how to be with horses, to train them yet still respect and honor them. Since that time, many amazing horses (and people) have come into my life to help me discover this balance. While I know I have many more lessons to learn from my equine friends, I also know my purpose is to share what I have already learned with others.

My goal in writing this book is to share with others the joy that is experienced by clearly and effectively communicating with horses. Whether you are a show rider, an endurance rider, a pleasure rider, or you simply enjoy spending time with horses, this book will offer you simple and straightforward concepts, exercises, and "tools" to create a unique toolbox, tailor-made by you. You may feel more drawn to some topics than others, and that's normal. Your intuition will guide you to focus on what's most important to you and your horse at the time. I recommend keeping this book close by, so that you can refer to it as you and your horse progress.

You'll notice that this book is not a how-to manual. I spent many years of riding instruction following directions and using my coach's tools with little thought as to why I was doing what I was doing. As I made the transition to becoming a professional horsewoman, I realized the importance of understanding the concepts behind why things were done a certain way. How liberating it was to be able to stay in the moment with a horse and adjust my methods to fit that horse's needs in that particular situation.

In any relationship, how you act and react depends on the individual you are in relationship with, as well as how each of you feels in that moment. This is also true in your relationships with horses. Understanding why different concepts and methods work will allow you to stay in the moment and find what works best for both you and the horse in this particular moment.

You will also become aware that this book focuses on both the horse and the human. It is equally important to understand how you are affecting the relationship as it is to understand your horse's perspective. True harmony is two beings moving as one, brought together by a mutual respect and appreciation for the individuality of one another. In the desire for a deep connection, it is important to recognize what is yours, what is mine, and what is ours. It is easy to either take on all the responsibility of the relationship, often experienced as self-blame or guilt, or to give all responsibility away, often expressing blame or feeling like a victim. This book will give you information and skills to aid you in holding both yourself and your horse accountable.

It is my intention to keep the topics simple and straightforward. Some of the most common compliments I receive when I am training or teaching are, "That's so simple, it just makes sense" or "it seems like such a small, simple thing, but it makes such a big difference." I hope you feel this way too after reading this book. I have included exercises to help you gain more insight into and clarification of certain topics. So now it's up to you. Read, enjoy, and have fun as you increase your equine communication skills.

Part 1: Introduction to Harmonious Horsemanship

One of my first rides on Willie. My sister, Samantha is riding Morag.

Chapter 1:
Horses and Humans

Why Horses?

My time in California was spent among horse people. I moved there because of horses, and almost everyone I met was a horse person. I became immersed in a world where horses were everywhere and working with them seemed to be a perfectly normal job. When I moved back to Canada and began meeting many non-horsey individuals, my job suddenly seemed anything but normal. Suddenly I was being asked questions about what I did that seemed simple yet provoked me to really look at my work. Rather than just going through the motions of being a horse person, I was reminded of why I chose to have horses in my life. I realized how common it is for horse people to become so accustomed to horses and how to be with them that much of the magic of just being with them is lost.

Whether or not horses would be in my life had never been a question; it was just a matter of what role they would play. As a child, horses lived in my imagination: in the books that I read, in my bicycle, in my "My Little Ponies," and in my dog, who learned to walk, trot, and canter on command. Their presence grew into Pony Club and weekly riding lessons and my first pony, Quantez. From there, my horses became my trusted partners in the jumper ring and my confidants in the barn. The relationships evolved into an education in horse psychology, equine body language, natural horsemanship, classical horsemanship as a rider, and interspecies communication. Horses became my work and once again my teacher as I began to study Equine Experiential Learning. How horses take part in my life continues to evolve. The only constant is their presence, their guidance, and their never-ending acceptance of who I really am.

There have been times in my life when I have felt overwhelmed and frustrated, saddened and sickened by the injustices I have witnessed to both horses and humans in the equine industry, both in the performance and natural horsemanship industries. I have seen horses abused both physically and emotionally, and soundness and health problems ignored and overlooked. I have seen horses stressed and scared, not knowing what a human is asking when the time is not taken to clarify or break the lesson down into steps. I have seen dominance misused both through aggressive and supposedly horse-friendly methods. I have witnessed drugs and equipment used as a replacement for training. I have seen riders shamed and degraded by trainers, and professionals choose money over integrity and pride over the welfare of the horse.

I have felt myself pulled off course, onto a path that is misaligned with my core beliefs of how we can be with these majestic animals. Yet often, in these moments when I least expect it, I have the privilege of watching a shared moment between horse and rider. In that moment, ego, fear, and injustice fall away and an indescribable feeling of peace and joy is present. When I am off track or discouraged, moments like these carry me forward, reminding me that awareness of a different way allows change.

A common misconception is that I share my work primarily for the horses. Horses are incredibly resilient, forgiving, and loving animals. They possess a wisdom that deserves to be honored and respected. Yet it is the human side of the relationship that drives me to educate. I know that I am most accepting and at peace with myself when I am around horses. I feel a deep sadness when I see someone struggling, rarely able to find these moments, even with his or her horse. I am saddened when the precious gifts of unconditional love and acceptance that horses offer are overlooked or remain unidentified as we so desperately seek approval, acceptance, recognition, and even status from other horse lovers. The desire to help people realign with why they were drawn to horses in the first place is my primary reason for sharing my knowledge. I believe if people remember "why horses?" the question will not be if they should learn how to have a deeper, more harmonious relationship with their horse. It will be, "How can I have a deeper, more harmonious relationship with my horse?"

The Simple Truth about Horses

The simple truth about horses is that they are willing, honest, and forgiving flight animals. They see us and accept us for who we really are and are amazingly adaptable to our human world. Imagine being dropped off in a place where no one spoke your language and everyone lived in a culture where customs and beliefs were very different from your own. Imagine the courage, determination, and willingness it would take to survive, adapt, and grow in that environment. This is what horses do every day in the human world.

As humans we have a tendency to overlook our horses' perspective. Horses have adapted so well to domestication and integrated themselves so fully into our daily lives that we sometimes forget another simple truth about them. Horses are not human. They are prey animals. They have four legs and a tail and often weigh ten times as much as we do. Their brains are a different size than ours and function and process information differently than ours do. They are flight animals, and their instinctual response to situations is often very different from our own. Yet despite these differences, horses and humans share an incredible bond.

By expanding our knowledge of horses and increasing our awareness of their perspective, we can create harmonious relationships based on trust and respect. By being conscious of ourselves and how we interact with our horses, we can deepen our communication with them and understanding of them. Problems that may have appeared complicated or unsolvable will be resolved with simple, straightforward solutions.

To truly understand our horses, we must educate ourselves about equine body language, the psychology of the horse, the autonomic nervous system of the horse, and interspecies communication. By understanding the mind, body, and spirit of the horse, we can communicate with the whole horse and recognize his or her individuality. Like humans, horses all have distinctive personalities and unique learning styles. By learning about each horse as an individual, we can make educated decisions on which training style is best suited to both our horses and ourselves.

Good Horsemanship Is Good Horsemanship

Good horsemanship is just that, good horsemanship. Today, as horse people, we have so many trainers, training methods, and types of horsemanship—both natural and traditional—available to us. Sometimes it can seem overwhelming as we look at everything available and try to decide who and what is correct and right for us and for our horses.

I have good news. There is more than one right answer. Horses, like humans, all have individual personalities and learning styles. The right trainer or method for you and your horse may differ from your neighbor, but that does not make either of you wrong. It's important to find what works best for you and your horse. Identifying your desires, your needs, and your definition of good horsemanship will help you find the right methods and trainers.

More and more, I see the gap between traditional and natural horsemanship being bridged. This brings me great joy as I am drawn to horses for their amazing spirit and the joy they bring me, yet the competitive side of me loves the sport of show jumping. For a long time I was under the wrong impression that I had to choose between the two. As I learned about natural horsemanship and interspecies communication, I found so much pleasure from the increased communication and harmony I felt with horses. I have now learned that this knowledge only enhances my experiences riding and jumping. Bringing together all that I have learned from the many talented instructors and trainers I have worked with over the years only allows me more tools to create a harmonious relationship with my equine partners.

Everyone has something to offer. I have learned a great deal from many trainers and teachers. Sometimes I have learned what I want to take as my own, and other times, I have learned what I want to leave out of my toolbox. Often what I chose to not use at the time for one horse pops into my head down the road to try with another, and it works. The contrast of all the different methods available allows us to discover what works for us and to grow as horse people. My toolbox is full of concepts, ideas, and knowledge from natural horsemen, traditional horsemen, dressage trainers, jumper riders, cowboys, Arabian horse trainers, race horse trainers, western riders, grooms, and the horses themselves. The method and equipment I use depends on what feels right for me and the horse in that moment.

An important piece of deciding what is right for you and your horse is finding methods and instruction that correspond with the individuality and learning style of both of you. Learning should seem easy, make sense, and feel good. This is also true for horses. At times you may have to push through resistance. You will know when you are on the right track when you realize that you are doing so in a relatively calm manner that leaves both you and your horse feeling better when you come out the other side of the issue.

Evolution is a fact of life. This is true for our relationships with our horses too. What worked yesterday may not work tomorrow. As your horse develops through his training process and as you grow as a rider, you will both be ready for new concepts and ideas. My first riding instructor did a great job of teaching me to post the trot, but I then needed to go to someone who specialized in the body language of the horse to really learn about body language. The people who taught me about body language were not the same people who taught me how to prepare a horse for the show ring. By identifying where I was and where I wanted to go, I became clear on what I needed from a trainer and/or a method of training. Think outside of the box, and be open to new concepts and ideas.

Each of us has a different perception of what good horsemanship is to us. My definition of good horsemanship is horsemanship that takes to heart the best interest of the horse and the human. It is creating a successful partnership through clear communication and understanding. It is about working in harmony with the animal, using trust, communication, and respect to create a happy, healthy, and willing equine partner. For me, any method incorporating these concepts is good horsemanship, whatever it may be labelled or whoever may be teaching it or putting it to use.

Chapter 2:
Communicating with Horses

🐎 🐎 🐎

The Secret to Communicating with Horses

All great clinicians, trainers, and riders, whether they use natural horsemanship or more traditional methods, have something in common. They have that undeniable connection with the horse, that thing we often refer to as "feel." They have it, and we watch it and want it too. So we buy the books and DVDs, attend clinics, workshops, and lessons, order the special equipment, sometimes even buy a horse from them, but often the methods just do not work for us. Some people seem to get it while others, no matter how much they practice, can't seem to make these methods work.

That's because most of the time an essential ingredient is missing—feel. I call it interspecies communication or the language of energy. Many trainers have it and use it but don't know how to describe it or teach it. For them, it just is; they feel it. They innately understand what the horse is feeling and what they need to do to create the relationship they desire. For me, it's something that has developed over time. We are all born with the ability to communicate through the language of energy, although we commonly lose our awareness of it as we mature and get caught up in our rational thoughts.

Not only are we born able to communicate through the language of energy, but also we still communicate that way every moment of every day whether we are aware of it or not. The language of energy is a language of emotion. This means every time we have a thought, it leads to an emotion. This emotion or feeling resonates though our own bodies and is transmitted out into the world. As well as sending our vibrations out into the world, we also receive the vibrations of other people. Have you ever noticed that you can feel a good or bad "vibe" about someone? What about when someone who is in a really bad mood enters the room? Do you notice the shift to a more negative mood in both yourself and others?

In our human world of conscious and rational thought, we often get so caught up in analyzing situations in our heads that we become less aware of how the situation is affecting how we are feeling or vibrating in our bodies. The portion of the horse's brain that deals with rational thought is significantly smaller than that of a human. This means that horses don't stand around thinking of what might happen or why something did happen. They stand in awareness of themselves and respond accordingly to whatever or whoever may enter their world.

Understanding interspecies communication is as important as understanding the body language of the horse and horse psychology. I have incorporated a number of ways you can improve your interspecies communication skills.

The Keys to Communicating with Horses

To achieve the highest level of communication with horses, we must communicate with their minds, bodies, and spirits. By creating harmony within our own minds, bodies, and spirits, we open the door for harmony in our relationships with horses. Communication is a meeting place for two beings to share their thoughts, perceptions, emotions, and experiences. It is equal parts sharing and listening. To arrive at communication in its purest form, we must know where we are, where the other party is coming from, and where we are meeting.

Keys to Communication

Interspecies Communication: Acknowledge where you are really at in the moment, and work forward from that place, wherever it may be. Horses communicate through felt sense rather than verbal communication. This means a horse will pick up on how you are feeling, not what you pretend to feel or would prefer to feel. For example, if you are getting ready to take your horse on your first trail ride together and you are feeling nervous, be honest with yourself about your nervousness. Your horse will pick up on your lack of confidence whether you want him to or not. Accepting that you are nervous will help you decide what tools you can use to assist you.

Horse Psychology: Recognize where your horse is at in the moment, understand his perspective, and acknowledge his individuality. For example, if you are taking your horse for his first trailer ride without his friends, be aware of how comfortable he is with the trailer, be aware that separating from his herd goes against his instincts, and be aware that he finds comfort from food. All these things will help you decide what tools can aid in making this experience as positive as possible for both you and your horse.

Equine Body Language: Meet them on common ground. Horses are living in our world of domestication, so help them understand our customs and way of life. Horses are always communicating through body language. By learning to communicate clearly and effectively with body language, humans can create safety, trust, leadership, and a place of comfort.

Chapter 3: Willingness

Change can be intimidating. As much as we want to learn a better way, leaving our comfort zone can be scary. This is the time when it is important to focus on your goals and desires. Below is a list of things to remind yourself to be open to on your journey to a more harmonious relationship with horses.

Be Willing to Be Uncomfortable

Feeling uncomfortable is good. It means you are trying something different, something new. When you were a baby learning to walk, crawling was a lot more comfortable than falling when you tried to walk. But you persevered, and look where you are now.

Our bodies have been programmed to act and react in a certain manner. Think of all the things your body does each day without you taking much notice. Driving, dialing a phone number, walking, talking, and picking out your horse's feet are all things that through practice and repetition you have programmed your body to do. It will take time for your body to learn new things, so be patient with yourself.

Conventional wisdom states that it takes twenty-one days to create a habit. Our minds, like our bodies, are also programmed to think in a certain way. Learning takes effort. Our minds must not only create a new way of thinking, but also remind our bodies of a new way of acting and reacting. This effort may seem uncomfortable, but it's worth it. Your mind and body will learn this new way of doing things, and when they do, it will seem as much a part of you as walking, talking, and cleaning your teeth.

A Lesson in the Benefits of Being Uncomfortable

One year I spent the winter and spring starting young horses, riding on my own and focusing on the horses. By summer, a number of the horses were ready to progress into the world of dressage, and I took them to a dressage trainer for lessons. Apparently my intense focus on the horses resulted in a lack of focus on myself. Some bad habits were the result, and luckily I had some very educated eyes to help me out. I regularly heard the phrases "look outside the ring" and "push your left arm forward" as we worked to straighten out my body and soften my contact on the left rein.

I remember trotting around the ring feeling awkward and just plain wrong as I pushed my left hand forward and looked out of the ring. But

I trusted the trainer and stuck with it. Soon I was able to feel more than just plain uncoordinated. I felt how straight the horses were going. Soon what had felt so wrong felt so right as the horses went better and better.

Be Willing to Be Emotional

Emotions will come up; it's natural. Horses see us for who we truly are no matter what image we project to the rest of the world. This can bring up our emotions as we look at pieces of ourselves we do not normally share with others, such as vulnerability, self-doubt, fear, hurt, anger, and many other pieces we keep hidden.

Emotional reactions such as tears or anger can release past trauma and allow room for growth. We often don't allow ourselves to react fully when our emotions arise and therefore hold onto them, pushing them down, at times even beating ourselves up over what we feel. While we strive to remain neutral when working with horses, not recognizing our emotions actually blocks neutrality. Like when a tree falls without a witness, if we feel an emotion but bury it so no one sees it, the emotion still exists.

When you find yourself feeling scared, angry, frustrated, uncomfortable, or sad, allow yourself to be present and feel the emotion. Emotions also have a message for us. For example, anger most often stems from fear for our safety and frustration at not having an answer. Remembering this will help you move through anger rather than lashing out at your horse or burying your rage.

Be Willing to Ask Questions

We are each in control of our own learning and responsible for our own education. Questions provoke thought, and thought provokes learning and growth. Question—ask why; understanding how and why certain things work will help select the tool in many situations, possibly in ways no one had thought of before. Ask your trainer, your farrier, your vet. Ask the barn manager, the grooms, your friend, the person who took the lesson you watched.

Be Willing to Feel

"Feel" is the freedom we experience when we are in harmony with ourselves and our horses. "Feel" comes when we remain present in the moment, present in our bodies, listening to our bodies and allowing them to respond. Feel often comes when our bodies and minds have learned something and are working together in harmony. It is common to expect to experience something in a certain way. Be aware of getting caught up in how you think it should feel, and thus missing the actual experience of feeling. Overthinking, overanalyzing, doubt, and fear are all things that block "feel."

A Lesson in Feel

I can remember clearly the first time I felt the body language of the horse. I had been at the Monty Roberts International Learning Center studying and learning about equine body language and had experienced it numerous times in the round pen, but I had yet to feel it. My experiences thus far had felt like clumsy attempts at speaking a foreign language. My timing was off as I interpreted it with my rational brain. It reminded me of learning Spanish and how I would hear a sentence in Spanish and then have to translate it into English in my head. I would then form my answer in English, once again translate, and finally respond in Spanish. After all my dreams of magical communications through the body language of the horse, I must admit I felt a little embarrassed and let down.

At the time, my horse Apollo was being boarded in pasture with a young Morgan stallion and a new addition, a dominant gelding. The stallion was normally very laid back and friendly but had been behaving territorially since the new arrival. Apollo was standing by himself, and I walked across the field with his halter while a friend waited for me just outside the pasture.

As I neared Apollo, I suddenly felt a strange sensation as my body reacted without any conscious direction from my brain. My body reacted by rapidly turning 180 degrees, getting very large and assertive, and stepping forward. Staring me in the face for a second before backing away was the young Morgan stallion. I was very excited as I turned to my friend. She quickly relayed her perspective on the situation.

She had watched as the young stallion approached me, not thinking much of it as he was normally fairly benign. When he was within a few feet from me, she recognized his territorial attitude and saw him raise his front leg to strike. She started to open her mouth to warn me as I suddenly turned to face the stallion in a very assertive posture. I had finally felt the body language of the horse, with no interpretation time needed.

These days I speak the body language of the horse fluently. My body can carry on a conversation with a horse while I have a discussion in English with the owner. Nowadays I actually have to put more effort into explaining a horse/human communication in English than I do to speak equine body language with the horse. Like learning anything new, there will be an uncomfortable time as your body and brain start to work in unison. Stick with it and know that soon it will be like brushing your teeth. You'll do it without thinking.

Be Willing to Make Mistakes

Mistakes are only an opportunity to learn. If we don't try things, we don't know if they work for us or if we like them. Every person is unique and has his or her own set of strengths, weakness, likes, and dislikes. When we are learning something new, we have to try things out to discover what works best for us and our horses. Furthermore, often what we classify as a mistake turns out to be a greater gift than we could imagine.

And Sometimes We Fall

When I was six years old, my family and I went to Scotland for the summer. My parents immigrated to Canada shortly after getting married, and most of our family was in Scotland and England. My mom had fond memories of riding through the Scottish Borders as a child and thought her hometown of Selkirk would be the perfect place to indulge my seemingly harmless obsession with horses.

My mom signed my sister and me up for riding lessons at a local stable called Dryden. After years of playing with "My Little Ponies" and dreaming of riding on a beautiful white pony, I was ecstatic. I felt like my dreams were coming true. My first lesson was on a white pony, Norseman. Norseman was a little shorter and shaggier than the pony of my dreams, but he was a Shetland after all. I have a picture of me getting back from my lead line ride through the hills with a grin stretching across my face, the luckiest girl in the world.

The next week when I arrived for my lesson, I discovered I had "graduated" to Willie, a slightly larger, dark bay pony. Once again I was in love. The next few lessons were spent in the arena learning to steer, stop, start, and even trot. I thought I had it all figured out and was very excited when it came time to go out for a country hack with Willie.

But sometimes we fall. It turned out Willie had a mind of his own when it came to the large open fields. Willie liked to canter, and to me it felt fast and out of control. Well, at least it did for the few seconds I stayed on. Things were not going quite as I had imagined. The summer was filled with falls. My record of three in a day still stands, and my memories of having Scottish thistle picked lovingly out of my legs remain strong. Yet I kept picking myself up and getting back on. I wanted to learn to ride so badly.

Willie and Norseman gave me one of the biggest gifts of my life. It took many years of falling and working through my fears for me to once again find the bliss I felt on Norseman that first day. With each lesson, I learned more and became a better rider. Today I realize how important my early riding years are to those who learn from me. I understand fear, I understand not being a natural from the start, and most of all, I understand the dream of that one blissful moment. I also understand that sometimes the important lessons come from what does not go as planned, not from what goes right.

I never know exactly where my next lesson will appear, and what I learn is so often deeper than the riding. I was working as an assistant trainer at a hunter/jumper barn and feeling very good about my skills as a rider. I was riding some of the nicest horses in the barn and loved the feeling when the horses seemed to dance under me. I rode a wide variety of horses, most of whom I adored. It's rare that I can't find something I love about a horse. Willie had taught me early to love what I rode, even if things didn't seem perfect.

Riley was different; we just didn't click. He was ridden regularly by another girl, one I was having problems working with. In fact, I harbored a fair amount of resentment toward his regular rider, whether she deserved it or not. But that day Riley was on my list. I was having a bad day. I had a lot going on in my personal life and was also starting to feel unfulfilled in my job. I was used to getting on horses and within a short period of time feeling them transform underneath me. I got on Riley and proceeded with my regular program, but he just stayed stiff. He was behind my leg, and the more I urged him forward the stickier he got. I was so aggravated. I knew about staying neutral and not taking things personally, but in that moment, I didn't care. I wanted him to listen to me.

And sometimes we fall. I tightly closed my legs on Riley's sides and smacked him with the whip behind my leg. Knowing how sensitive horses are to our emotions, I'm sure the zing from my anger was stronger than the smack from my whip. Riley reared up, and I came down, hard. My elbow broke my fall. I jumped up even more furious, grabbed his reins, and smacked him on the neck. He pulled back and tore away from me, down the hill. Another trainer asked if I was okay as I ran after him, and all I said was, "I'm so mad right now I can't tell. I'll let you know in a few minutes." And that was the truth.

I caught Riley and realized I had to calm down before I got on or I would just end up back in the dirt. I got back on and finished my ride, taking the time to ask Riley rather than demand from him. By the time I got off, my elbow had a huge bump on it. In the waiting room of the hospital, I had plenty of time to reflect on my mistakes and come to terms with the shame of how I acted. I was forced to look at why I hadn't remained neutral as well as the anger and frustration I was feeling in many areas of my life.

Riley has been one of my greatest teachers about how making mistakes and falling can lead to growth. After my fall from Riley, my life didn't miraculously improve; however, my horse work did as I learned to leave my anger in the tack room. I started to look inside myself at many things I didn't want to see. I was feeling disillusioned with the show world, or at least my place in it.

I'm a perfectionist. I love the show world for the opportunity it holds for me to perfect my riding ability and to explore the subtleties of communication between horse and rider. I can spend endless hours discovering the intricacies taken to influence the powerful energy of the horse underneath me. The horses I had the opportunity to ride were incredible, high-quality animals.

Yet I was torn. I saw horses being misunderstood, being treated as vehicles rather than living beings. More often than not, I believe it is not people's intention to purposefully abuse a horse. However, the rampant misuse and overuse of drugs and equipment are harmful and abusive. I saw horses distressed, scared, and acting out as their social and individual needs and personalities were not met. Dominance and even aggression were used to correct the undesirable behavior. I saw horses slipping through the cracks both mentally, emotionally, and physically because humans were more focused on the end result, a ribbon or championship, than on the well-being of the horse. I knew it didn't need to be that way. I just wasn't sure what to do about it. In truth, a part of me was unsure if I wanted to do anything about it. There were so many horses and people that I cared about at the barn and so many things that I loved about the show world. I was doing all I could within the situation, but it still didn't feel like enough.

Roughly a month after my fall, Riley colicked. It became serious quickly. By evening, he was in extreme pain and past the point of surgery.

Various miscommunications had led to Riley being in much more pain than necessary. The decision was made to put him down. I was angry. I felt like Riley had not been given a fair chance. He had experienced various mild colics in the months leading up to this one. I felt more could have been done earlier, that his well-being should have been top priority, that his death could have been prevented, that Riley had suffered much more than necessary, and that he had not been seen for the incredible being he was.

But sometimes we rise. The lesson Riley had taught me just a month earlier turned into action. I put my anger aside. I felt Riley needed to be supported as he left our world, that he deserved to have someone by his side who cared about and respected him. I knew being with him was too painful for his regular rider. I chose to be there with him, to give back to him as he had given to me. I was very glad we both made that choice. I have been there for this transition for a number of horses, but this was the most traumatic for me. Riley fought the drugs; he hung on to life for as long as he could. My heart broke for Riley that night. It broke for all the horses that deserved better. It was that night I knew that I could no longer turn a blind eye and overlook all the injustice I saw in the horse industry.

When I left Riley, I went to his rider and gave her a hug and told her how sorry I was. I could imagine the pain she must have been feeling.

I honored Riley's life by honoring his profound bond with her. My heart was full of compassion as I acknowledged her pain and her love for Riley.

The same horse who had thrown me to the ground had pushed me up as I realized the gifts that come when I open my heart and rise above my own ego. That night as I drove to see my own pony, Breeze, my anger gave way to sadness, and instead of shame, I felt proud. Proud of the person I was becoming.

Be Willing to Trust the Process

Life's greatest gifts come from the journey, not the end result. This is also true in our relationship with horses. Having a goal is important, but remaining in the present moment is even more important. The process of growth and change is not always easy or comfortable, but if we trust in the process, the lessons that we learn and the gifts we receive will be greater than we could ever imagine.

My Journey

I always knew that I wanted to work with horses. As I neared the end of high school, I started to look at horses as a career. I could not imagine much else. The September after graduation I started working as a groom at Spruce Meadows. I was soon riding a number of horses daily as well as mucking stalls, feeding, and grooming horses. The days were long, but I was learning a ton. I had regular lessons with Albert Kley and developed a whole new appreciation for flat work and schooling horses. But I was unhappy. I was homesick, not sure how to deal with politics between fellow grooms, and most of all, I missed the connection I had always enjoyed with my own horses. Not having hours to spend grooming and riding each horse, I didn't know how to connect with them. After four months, I decided to head home. One month later, I started to travel, feeling discouraged about my dream of becoming a horse trainer.

After two years of travelling, I was still feeling uninspired and unhappy with my life when I heard of some interspecies communication workshops being offered in my area. A friend had taken them and thought I would love them. I did. After attending numerous workshops, learning about the language of energy, and learning how understanding myself better helped me connect more deeply with animals, I bought a ten-month-old horse named Apollo. I explored my newfound knowledge with Apollo and once again found joy from my connection with a horse.

As Apollo reached two years old, I was once again feeling at a bit of a loss. I dreamed of showing him and jumping him but felt there was something missing between the work I had been doing and the work I wanted to do. A friend reminded me of Monty Roberts, and I signed up for a clinic. One clinic turned into the Monty Roberts Introductory Course, the Monty Roberts Instructor Course, and then time spent at Flag Is Up Farm teaching Join-Up clinics, Follow-Up clinics, and introductory courses. For four years I was inspired as both a student and an instructor by the body language and psychology of the horse. It added another layer of connection to the inter-species communication I was already using.

As time went on, while I appreciated all that I had learned, I realized that I preferred taking more time developing the subtleties of the communication. I still believed that the horse/human relationship could be taken to an even deeper level, one that held in it even more respect and connection. I was also being taught by a pony name Breeze that I was pushing through my insecurities instead of dealing with them. It was time to explore all I had learned about body language and behavior in a different way.

I wanted to feel the same connection riding a horse that I felt in the round pen. A casual trail ride didn't do it; my passion was jumping. My horse Apollo had soundness issues that caused me to find him a more suitable home, and I started looking for a job where I could educate myself as a rider. Soon I found a job riding and teaching at an "A" circuit hunter/jumper barn. I felt like the luckiest person around. I spent my days riding very nice show horses and getting regular lessons with amazing trainers. My riding improved by leaps and bounds, and I was soon able to bring along horses while experiencing that connection that I had been searching for. I was doing very little ground work, but while I was riding, I was playing around with the concepts that I had learned in my studies of horse psychology, equine body language, and interspecies communication.

After two years riding and teaching, I again found myself disillusioned. I often felt that with all my knowledge I could bring more to the table for these animals. I felt confined in someone else's business. I had so many ideas on how I could bring together all I knew about horses and horse training to make things better for them. I needed the freedom to do things my way, even if that meant making mistakes or taking extra time. It was a scary time for me as I realized it was time to start my own business.

I started up Harmonious Horsemanship, offering services such as horse starting, behavior consults, and lessons. Finally bringing together all the knowledge, my past experiences, and standing true to my own beliefs was a journey in itself. The horses and clients I work with constantly add clarity and insight into the work I do and the direction I want to take. Since starting Harmonious Horsemanship, I have continued to educate myself and learn where I can grow more. As working with horses became second nature, I realized the value I gained by being part of the human experience in behavior consults and lessons. I noticed how my clients changed as their horses did.

My more recent adventures include learning more about humans. I am a self-proclaimed workshop junkie, enjoying attending workshops on personal growth and development as well as leadership. Not only do I enjoy learning about myself, I enjoy watching how these workshops are taught, how people learn, and which pieces affect which people the most. I have attended a training course on equine experiential learning as well as working one on one with clinical counsellor and Advanced Epona instructor Deborah Marshall. The self-regulation and trauma release work Deborah does with humans clarified a lot of the work I was doing with horses intuitively. The deeper understanding I gained behind the science of self-regulation and trauma has allowed me to take my work with traumatized horses to a whole new level.

Once again as I add new concepts and tools to my toolbox, my connection with both horses and people is deepened and strengthened. As graduation approached and I decided I was going to work with horses, I could never have imagined the journey that lay before me. At times I felt lost and unhappy, but as I focused on what I wanted to do, I course-corrected and found the next lesson available to me. As I started to feel complete in my journey with the horses, I realized the next journey lay with the horses and their humans. The most amazing thing to me is that in my journey to find a way to work with horses and experience a strong bond, I now experience a greater connection with horses as well as with humans than I could ever have imagined.

Be Willing to Accept Gifts

While many people talk about true partnership and fifty/fifty partnership with horses, many do not allow themselves to fully experience it. In the modern horse industry, it is easy to get caught up in what we want from our horses, what we can train them to do, and what kind of life we can provide for them. As we focus on ourselves, the true meaning of partnership is overlooked, and the gifts our horses are willing to share are overlooked.

Horses offer us the gifts of unconditional love, acceptance, interaction with us in terms of who we really are, and insight into the pieces of ourselves we often hide from others. The lack of ego in horses and their present-moment focus offer us many insights and lessons to help us become more aligned with who we really are and more in tune with the world around us. If we can pause for a moment and recognize horses as true equals, the gifts they offer become clear. We then just have to willingly accept them.

Part 2: Interspecies Communication

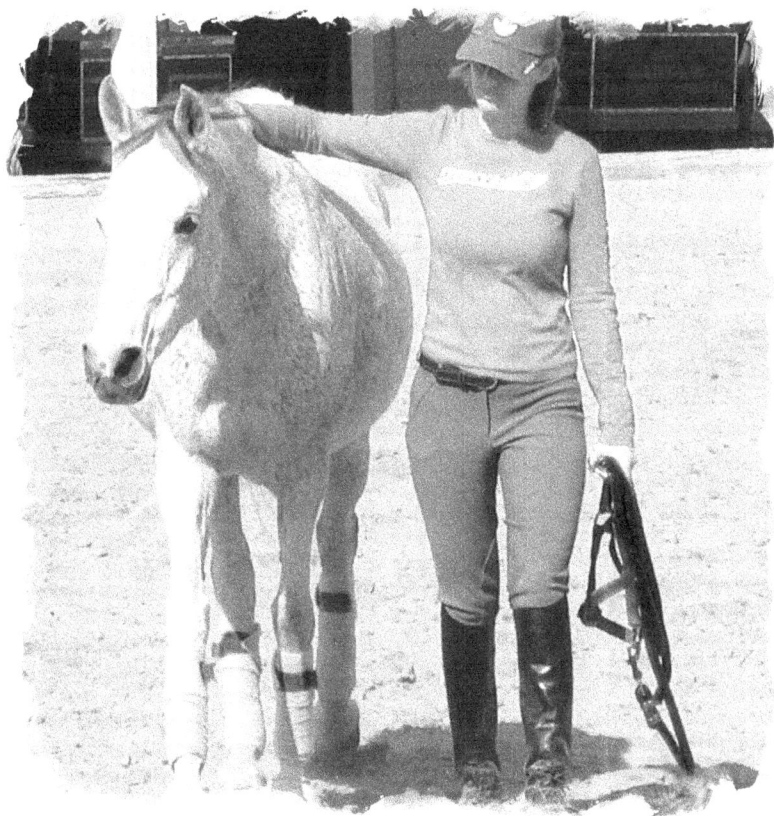

Breeze and I enjoying a quiet moment together.

Chapter 4:
Breeze: Lessons in Authentic Communication

I believe every person and horse comes into our lives for a reason. I also believe that we get the lessons we need, not necessarily the ones we want. This was the case with a sensitive, beautiful, and often opinionated American Sports Pony named Breeze. At the time I met Breeze, I was making some changes in my life and trying to gain some clarity on what direction to go in the horse industry. I thought a project horse might bring me extra income and give me something to do. A client called me to let me know a pony that she had been boarding was being donated to UC Davis and would be picked up in the morning unless I wanted her. That's when I found Breeze.

When I went to see Breeze that evening, it was clear that she was very nervous, did not trust people, and was not interested in building a relationship with me. In the cross ties when I got her ready, she could not stand still and even raised her hind leg when I approached her hind end. When I took her in the round pen to lunge her, she flew around at top speed with her tail in the air. Finally, when I got on her, she reared and refused to go forward. After a few minutes, I was able to get her going and jump her round a 2'6" course. Although she was wiggly and green under saddle, she jumped well and was actually quite fun. Unsuitable as she was as a kid's pony, I still took her, thinking I would be able to help her learn to trust people, find a good home, and make me a profit in the process. Little did I know that the gifts Breeze would bring me would be much more powerful and important than a few extra dollars.

Once Breeze arrived, I expected her behavior to turn around quite quickly. But Breeze had other plans. She had no intentions of working with me, and all her negative experiences with people were fresh in her mind. I only knew a few facts about Breeze's history. She was eight years old when she came into my life. She had already had four babies, which, you can imagine, means she was bred for the first time when she was still a baby herself. She had been started at some point either before or between foals. She was a good mom. She had a very hard time being separated from her last foal.

Over the years, Breeze would share her side of the story. She told me of a young pony who was handled with little understanding of her sensitive nature. She told me of not understanding what her rider wanted, being scared and tense with her head tied down and her mouth always being pulled on. She revealed a fear of horses leaving her, just as her foals had. She told me of not knowing or understanding the human world or what humans wanted. Breeze informed me of the confusion a horse feels when a human acts one way but feels another. She taught me the trauma this can cause a horse, how humans can be abusive to horses simply by not listening and by not being aware.

Although I was aware of interspecies communication before Breeze came into my life, she took me beyond selective use of it and into living it. Breeze's highly sensitive nature meant only if I was congruent could I be clear in my communications. Perhaps it was because she was my pony, or maybe because we are similar in nature, but either way, Breeze related to me on a deeper level than other horses and people. In fact, she forced me to look at myself in ways that often made me very uncomfortable. Breeze was a bit like the school of hard knocks. I learned my lessons either way. Sometimes it was the hard way, but when things went right, they went really right.

My relationship with Breeze was far from idealistic. We made mistakes, experienced anger and sadness, faced our fears, and learned to open our hearts to each other. During our time together, there were many times I wanted to give up, thought I was the wrong person for her, seriously considered selling her, and felt lost and frustrated. At the same time, we shared a deep connection, experienced great joy, and never gave up on each other. This rocky path created the opening for us to heal each other and find our true paths.

Breeze reminded me of my love for horses and kept me grounded at a time when the flash of the show world made me question my ethics and idealism. I exposed Breeze to a human world that was more understandable and introduced her to the love (and carrots) that people can bring. When I was ready to stand true to who I was and Breeze was ready to share all her gifts, our paths separated.

I moved back to Canada to start Harmonious Horsemanship while Breeze stayed in California with my friend Jen. Although Jen bought Breeze for herself, it quickly became apparent that Breeze wanted to be a kid's pony. This worked out well as Jen loved teaching kids and had dreamed of her own riding school. Breeze became the first school pony at Jen's Punk Pony Riding School. I recently went to visit and felt honored to see this amazing pony jumping around a course with a young girl and, later, babysitting a beginner rider.

As I was watching Breeze in her jumping lesson, another pony bucked his rider off. He went for a mad gallop, bucking around the ring and doing flybys past the other horses. It took us quite a few minutes to catch him, and all the while Breeze stood calmly watching, her rider safely on her back. I realized then just how far Breeze had come, a long way from the pony I went to look at many years ago. I am so grateful that Jen is able to give Breeze the chance to share her life with so many kids while allowing her the freedom to be the unique individual that she is.

Breeze is a pony that changes lives. I feel privileged that my life has been so touched by hers. Her life these days may seem like the average life of any school pony, but that is not the case. Her ability to see people for exactly who they are, combined with her strong and definite opinions, caused her a great deal of pain early in her life. But for those who allow Breeze to be herself, she has so much to offer. I am extremely grateful for all the lessons Breeze not only shared with me but with the many highly sensitive horses I have met since. Breeze shared with me the harm humans can do simply by not listening and by not being clear within themselves. Even more importantly, Breeze is an inspiring example of a pony's resilience and capacity to heal.

Chapter 5:
What Is Interspecies Communication?

The Language of Energy: A Felt Language

All animals, including human beings, are born with an innate ability to understand and communicate with each other. Interspecies communication is facilitated through the language of energy, which is best described as a felt, or internal, language rather than a verbal or body language. Wild animals are very in tune to this language of energy as it is essential for their survival, while humans are often so focused on verbal language that we have lessened our awareness of the language of energy. By returning our focus to our feelings and body sensations, we can increase our knowledge and awareness of interspecies communication. Understanding our emotions and being clear on our intentions are great ways to start the process.

Whether predator or prey, most animals respond instinctually to their environment. They are in tune with the balance of energy both in themselves and their environment. When there is a shift in energy, as in when a predator enters the pasture where horses are grazing, the horses will simultaneously feel the shift in energy in both themselves and their environment and respond accordingly. Unlike humans, animals rely on this felt sense rather than rational thoughts.

The language of energy is a felt language, meaning it is best interpreted by recognizing our internal sensations in response to an outer stimulus. For those of us who are not in tune with this felt sense, some questions may arise: What was the shift in energy? What did the horses feel? Take a moment to relax, take a few deep breaths, and imagine a beautiful sunny day. Imagine you are with your loved ones in a serene and familiar environment. All of you are on the same wavelength, enjoying a peaceful and tasty meal together. Picture someone who is driven and tense, pumping with adrenaline, entering your serene setting. How does your body react? Remember to focus on your body, the sensations you are feeling, not on your thoughts. Likely your body started to mirror that of the one who entered, by tensing, with heart rate and adrenaline increasing. This is what happens to the horses. Feeling the shift in themselves, they react accordingly.

While humans are born with the same abilities as all other animals for communicating through the language of energy, we often are so reliant on verbal language that our awareness of inter-species communication is pushed aside. Verbal language deals much more with rational thought than felt sense. This may be explained by the fact that a significant difference between humans and other animals is the proportion of the human brain devoted to the neocortex, which deals with rational thought. We learn to interpret and rationalize our emotions, our bodies' reactions, and our feelings, and in doing so, often get so caught up in thought that we miss the message our bodies are sharing with us. We often end up saying what we think we should say rather than what we feel.

Horses, like most animals, are very in tune with the language of energy. They do not hear the words we are saying to ourselves or others but rather what we are feeling. To use inter-species communication to our advantage, we must first recognize what we are communicat-ing. A great way to monitor how we are truly feeling, which is also what we are communi-cating, is to be aware of our emotions. Take time to be honest with yourself about how you are feeling and then be aware of the sen-sations in your body that coincide with your emotions. By spending a small amount of time each day being aware of your emotions and your body's sensations just as they are, you will quickly become reconnected with the felt lan-guage of energy.

Exercise 1: Body Scan

The practice of doing a body scan on a regular basis is a great way to bring your awareness into your body and into the present moment. Once your awareness has shifted inward, it will become easier to recognize the emotions you are feeling as well as what message they may have to share with you. Doing a body scan just takes a moment yet is a valuable tool in self-awareness and inter-species communication. It's a great way to start your session with your horse as well as being a check-in tool throughout your session. Sometimes during a body scan, an emotion or knowing may come up. If this happens, take the time and just observe it.

Find a quiet place where you will not be interrupted. Stand with your feet underneath you, roughly shoulder width apart. Close your eyes or soften your gaze down toward the ground. Take a moment to notice your breath, just as it is. Notice when the in breath changes into out breath. Starting at the top of your head, slowly bring your attention down to your body and notice how you are feeling. Notice what areas are comfortable, what feels relaxed. Notice any areas of tension or discomfort. Just notice—there is no need to change anything. Take your time and scan your whole body, from your head down to your feet. If your attention feels drawn to a particular spot, allow it to focus there for a moment as you breathe in and out. When you are ready, continue scanning the rest of your body. When your scan is complete, slowly open your eyes, allowing the light to seep in.

The Language of Energy: Emotion and Intention

The language of energy could also be called the language of emotion and intention. This is how horses are able to sense when you are scared or angry, happy or sad. Have you ever noticed when you are in a very bad mood, your horse reacts over-dramatically? Or when you are nervous, your horse starts to become nervous and spooky? Or when you are only asking your horse to do something because you think you should, and your horse won't do it? This is because energy is a language of emotion and intention, and your horse is reading your emotions and intentions and reacting accordingly.

By simply being aware that your emotions and intentions can affect how you convey information to your horse, you can improve how you communicate with her. You can learn to use your energy and intent to aid you in achieving your goals with your horse. Remember, horses don't speak English, so they hear what you are feeling not what you are saying. Being honest with yourself about how you are feeling will help create a stronger bond between you and your animal and, in certain situations, will give you more options for solving problems.

There is a difference between horses and humans when it comes to dealing with emotion. Horses understand that emotions have a message. They feel the emotion in their bodies, accepting whatever they feel. Horses innately know what message each emotion brings, and they react accordingly. Humans have a tendency to focus on the story they associate with the emotion, bringing the emotion from their bodies into their minds. With emotions such as anger, sadness, and fear that at times can be uncomfortable, many humans try to push it down or ignore it. When the message attached to the emotion is ignored, the emotion tends to hang around and wait for an opportunity to be heard, often even intensifying until it is heard. If you are interested in learning more about the messages your emotions have to share, I recommend reading *Riding Between the Worlds* by Linda Kohanov.

The following sections will introduce you to some easy ways that you can work on your interspecies communication skills. Breathing, positive thinking, stating your intention, visualization, singing, and listening to your intuition are all examples of how you can use awareness and energy to assist you.

Chapter 6: Positive Thinking

Positive thinking is essential when working with horses. Horses are very intuitive animals. They are very in tune with their environment as well as with the humans they interact with. Whatever we are focusing on, our horses will understand through our energy, intentions, emotions, and physical body and respond to it accordingly. Through awareness of our thoughts, we can become confident, positive leaders.

Stating Your Intention

A horse looks for a calm, assertive leader to guide him and help him live a long and healthy life. Below are two statements. Which one would you derive confidence from?

1. We are walking calmly and quietly past the garbage cans.
2. Those garbage cans look scary. I hope he doesn't spook or buck.

Our bodies resonate with our thoughts. In the first statement, we are creating a scenario to be walking calmly and quietly; thus our bodies are relaxed, our heart rates are down, our breathing is normal, and our minds are open. In the second statement, we are creating a fearful, scary situation with possible spooking or bucking. If we feel this way, our bodies will tense, our heart rates and breathing will increase, and our minds will close as our sympathetic nervous system is activated. Our horses will mirror us in both positive and negative ways. Even if we are feeling apprehensive, by focusing on what we do want instead of what we don't, we can start to change our own reactions. The more we practice this the easier it gets.

Imagine that your horse, as well as your body, only responds to the key words in a sentence. Read through the following statements, and choose the key words in each. Are the key words creating a positive or a negative intention?

- My horse walks right into the trailer. He is a great loader.
- My horse always stops at the water jump. He never goes over it.
- I hope my horse doesn't spook at the barking dogs.
- Those bushes look kind of scary. He spooked at something like that before.
- I am going to ride into the ring confidently, and we are going to go over all the jumps the first time.

A Lesson in Thoughts and Intention

Among her many lessons, Breeze taught me about the power of positive thinking. Unfortunately, this was one of the lessons I gained clarity on through contrast. During our first six months together, Breeze started to learn boundaries, learn to control her body, and learn to self-regulate (more on these topics later). The rearing had quickly stopped within our first week together, but when she was scared under saddle, she had a tendency to bolt. This had been a trigger for me since the days of Willie. Bolting actually frightened me more than bucking or rearing.

One day when I was riding Breeze in the ring, something spooked her, and she bolted across the ring. Although we were alone in a large ring, this triggered an old fear, and unwanted thoughts started popping into my head. I was not going to fall off like when I was a kid on Willie, but I started thinking of all that could go wrong. Soon I started thinking, "What if she runs into the fence? Please don't run into the fence."

Now, you'll remember how sensitive Breeze was to my thoughts, feelings, and emotions. In her state of fear, she responded to me, and *crash*! We hit the fence. This was a very clear example of how my body transmitted my thoughts straight to Breeze. Luckily Breeze was not hurt, and I just suffered from a sore knee and wounded pride.

Interestingly enough, as I learned skills to help me work through my fear of her bolting and was able to think about being able to stop her, her reactions dissipated. Soon the behavior disappeared. On my recent trip to visit Breeze, I was able to see she still requires the same sense of clarity from her riders. As a beginner rider walked and attempted to trot around the top half of the ring, it wasn't until the little girl became clear and committed to what she wanted that Breeze obliged.

It is important to mention that there may be times when you feel you cannot think positively or create a positive affirmation. Please honour this, slow the process down and consider if there is a fear or trauma that needs to be further explored. As you read on you will find more information about both these topics.

Exercise 2: Creating a Positive Affirmation

Here is a great exercise to use before and during your time with your horse:
Before you start a session with your horse, take a moment to breathe and think about your goals for the session (see "Goal Setting" on page 174). Create a *positive* affirmation stating your intentions for the session. Think about what you do want to achieve rather than what you don't want to happen. If you find yourself thinking in the negative, swap it around. For example, if

you do not want your horse to be spooky and jumpy, you likely want him to be quiet, calm, and relaxed. From this a positive affirmation is, "We are enjoying a calm and quiet ride." Repeating your affirmation a few times will help you to be clear and confident about your intention. This clarity and confidence will transfer to your horse as well as help you to remain calm and open to new ideas. If you find yourself getting tense or frustrated during your session, breathe and repeat your affirmation as often as you need to. Our relationships with our horses are equal partnerships. This means your affirmation can be about you, your horse, or, best of all, both of you as a team. Play around and have fun with this.

Chapter 7: Breathing

Breathing and Our Bodies

Breathing is an essential part of life. We do it all day, every day. How we breathe affects our bodies and our minds. It also affects how others, both animal and human, respond to us. When we are calm and relaxed, we take long, deep breaths, our heart rate is normal, and our minds are open to learning and processing information. When we become nervous or scared, our bodies tense, we take shallow, rapid breaths, our heart rates increase, and it becomes more difficult to be open to receiving and processing information.

By being aware of your breathing and deliberately taking long, deep breaths, you can bring your adrenaline level down, slow your heart rate down, relax your body, and open your mind to learning and processing information. This is a great tool for new or "scary" situations. It is also helpful if you find yourself feeling frustrated or angry. Horses not only feel the physical effect fear and frustration have on your body, but also they sense your emotions. Consciously choosing to take long, deep breaths will help relax your body and shift your mood. This will make your time with your equine partner more enjoyable as well as help you be the calm, confident leader your horse is looking for.

An Early Lesson in the Benefits of Breathing

Every summer when I was in high school, our local hunter/jumper club hosted a two-day show. We had Victor Hugo Vidal, a renowned trainer and judge, come up to judge the show and give a clinic in the days leading up to it. Victor was my favorite clinician. My horse and I always seemed to be at our best by the end of the clinic, and the timing was great. After our show, I would head off to some "A" circuit shows on the mainland.

One word stands out to me when I remember these summer clinics—*breathe*. During every clinic with every rider, Victor would remind us of the importance of breathing as we rode. As we took turns jumping the exercises he had laid out for us, he would again remind us individually to breathe. At the time, I did not understand why he wanted us to breathe. I just knew my horse's way of going improved, and I noticed the other horses and riders relax and enjoy their ride.

There are many great breathing exercises you can practice on a daily basis. I suggest working on your breathing away from the barn as well as at the barn. By practicing taking deep, relaxing breaths in a calm environment, it will become second nature. This way when you find yourself in a tense or stressful situation at the barn, or anywhere else for that matter, you'll only have to consciously take a few deep breaths, and your mind and body will immediately start to respond.

Exercise 3: Breathing

Find yourself a comfortable place to sit or lie down if you haven't already done so. You may want to use pillows and blankets for added support so that you can relax even more. Sitting or lying quietly, settle in, relax your body, and close your eyes. Make any adjustments you need to make, letting your hands rest in your lap or comfortably at your sides, allowing any tension you may be holding to gently let go. As you continue to relax your body, noticing how it feels, bring your attention to your breath. As you breathe in and breathe out, notice the rise and fall of your chest with each inhale and exhale, and feel your body relax even more. Slowly bring your attention to the moment when your "in" breath becomes an "out" breath, feeling the temperature of your breath as it enters your body and as it leaves. With each new "in" breath, feel your body filling with life, and with each "out" breath, letting go of all that you no longer need. Slowly allow your breath to deepen, welcoming even more life into your body, allowing yourself to relax. As your chest rises and falls, continue to deepen your breathing, filling your entire body with this life-giving breath. Feel the gentle rhythm of your breathing like a silky ribbon flowing in and through your arms, your legs, your belly, from the top of your head to the tips of your fingers and toes, feeling the sensations of your body filled with life.

When you're ready, slowly allow your breathing to return to your normal rhythm and pace, taking a moment to notice how you're feeling now. Allow any sensations you may be feeling to just be there as you begin to bring your attention back into the room. Feel your body supported by the chair or floor, wiggle your fingers and your toes, stretch, and move your body, noticing the sounds around you, and when you're ready, slowly open your eyes.

Singing

Sometimes we find ourselves in a situation where it feels difficult to change our thought patterns, think positively, and keep breathing. Although we know what we should do to be the confident leaders our horses are looking for, it can sometimes be hard to do it. This is when I sing. Yes, sing, either in my head or out loud. Singing serves many purposes to help us overcome our old patterns and fears, including having a more positive experience. Singing was one of the tools I used to work through my fear of Breeze bolting.

Singing forces you to breathe. This in turn relaxes your body, helps your heart rate and breathing remain normal, and helps keep your adrenaline down. Singing also changes any negative thought patterns you may be having. If you are busy singing the words to a song, it is difficult to think about your fears. Sing a happy song, and you will feel your mood lighten. It's hard to be mad when you are singing a happy song. It's better to be neutral than negative. Singing is a great tool to help keep you neutral.

Chapter 8: Visualization

Supporting Your Intentions

Visualization is a tool that many top athletes, including riders, use to improve and get the best out of their performance. By creating a mental model of a situation or event, and going over it in our minds while in a relaxed state, we can increase the likelihood that the situation will play out according to our desired outcome.

The human body does not distinguish between an event that is experienced and an event that is imagined vividly. Through visualization, we can create neurological patterns that then lead to muscular response. With repeated and deliberate visualization, we can strengthen the associated pattern in the nervous system, which makes the imagined responses more likely to occur in the actual situation.

Visualization is not only for competitors. It can be used to aid in working through fears, learning new skills, and improving everyday situations. All it takes is a little bit of time and repetition. The more you visualize the situation or event, the more you strengthen the pattern in your body as well as becoming clearer and more vivid in your imagining.

If you don't immediately see clear and vivid pictures when you start visualizing, be kind to yourself. It's normal and will improve the more you practice. The important thing is creating the mental model in your mind.

Sadie: A Lesson in the Benefits of Visualization

A few years ago, I was starting a young mare named Sadie. During the time of her training, Sadie was growing and changing shape. She reminded me of a gawky teenager that was all legs and had no idea what to do with her body. She was comfortable cantering under saddle but had trouble picking up her left lead. If she picked it up, she was quite comfortable, but she had a hard time figuring out how to position her body for the transition into it. To make matters worse, the left is my weaker direction, so my aids were not as clear as they were on the right. The more I worried about her picking up the wrong lead, the tenser I became and the more I interfered with her natural body positioning.

While I knew what I needed to do to help her pick up the left lead, I was having a hard time getting my weaker side to do what I wanted it to. I decided to try visualizing riding Sadie. Every night for about ten minutes I would lie down and visualize my ride the following morning. I focused on the trot I would need to prepare her for the canter transition. I imagined myself doing just what I needed to do with my body to pick up the left lead. I saw Sadie, relaxed and happy, picking up the left lead.

I started my nightly ritual of visualizing Sadie and me successfully picking up the left lead at the beginning of the week. By the end of the week, we were doing it almost as well as I had visualized. The best part was that I did not have to work hard at being in the right position. I just had to relax, think about it in my mind, and allow my body to react accordingly.

Using a Key Word

Visualization can also be abstract. With every thought you think or imagine, a physical response is occurring at some level. Sometimes you can have trouble visualizing a real-life scenario because the thought of the situation creates anxiety in your mind and body. When this happens, it's best to recognize what you would like to experience in this situation. After you are clear on this, you can find another visualization that will allow you to experience the desired response. I recommend using a key word that describes the sensation you are aiming for, to associate with the visualization and desired response. The more you practice the visualization, the stronger your body's response to the key word and the visualization. Now you can take the key word to your real-life scenario and use it to prompt your body to respond in the desired manner.

Exercise 4: "Grounding" as a Key Word

The following is an exercise I use to bring myself into the present moment, especially at times when I find myself nervous, anxious, or anticipatory. I use the key word "grounding" to bring about the same "grounded" feelings I associate with doing this exercise.

Find a safe, comfortable place to stand, with your feet firmly placed beneath you, legs shoulder width apart. Relax your body, close your eyes, and take a few deep breaths, feeling the air flow in and out of your body. As you continue to relax into a comfortable standing position, bring your attention to the place where your feet are connected with the earth, and feel the earth beneath you. Imagine that you have roots reaching out from your feet growing down into the earth. Noticing how deep they go, imagine and feel how they branch out, connecting you with the earth. Notice how much earth is beneath you, how much you are connected to and a part of the earth. Know that these roots can and do move with you, keeping you grounded wherever you go. Breathe in, feeling grounded and supported, and let this feeling settle into your body.

Take a few more deep breaths, and when you're ready, slowly open your eyes. Take a moment to savor and enjoy this feeling of being grounded and calm, knowing you can take this with you, wherever you go, as you move on with your day.

Exercise 5: Guided Visualization for Presence and Connection

Find a quiet and comfortable spot to sit or lie down if you haven't already done so. You may want to use pillows and blankets to allow yourself to relax even more. I invite you to settle in, relax your body, and close your eyes. Lying down or sitting comfortably, make any adjustments you need to make, letting your hands come to rest in your lap or at your side, allowing any tension you may be holding to gently let go. Take a deep breath, hold it, and exhale with a deep sigh. Take another deep breath, hold it, exhaling with an audible sigh, and one more deep breath, hold it, and exhale, allowing a deep wave of relaxation to flow through your body. Your whole body is relaxed.

Gently bring your attention to your breath, noticing the rise and fall of your chest as you breathe in and breathe out, and observe where your inhale turns into an exhale. Continuing to relax, allow your breathing to deepen, feeling the temperature of your breath as it flows in and then out of your body. As you inhale, feel your breath entering and filling your body, and as you exhale, let all unnecessary thoughts and tension flow out of your body. Allowing your body to relax, feel the support of the chair or the surface beneath you.

Imagine you are in a safe place, a horsey place, and there is a horse waiting for you. You may know this horse already, or you may not. What does the horse look like? Feel like? Smell like? What color is he or she? Does this horse have a name? If so, what is it? If you haven't already done so, take your time and approach the horse. Reach out and touch him or her. How does his or her coat feel beneath your fingers? Allow your hands to move, touching and feeling this beautiful animal. Notice whatever you are feeling, just observing any emotions you may be experiencing as they arise.

Continuing to relax, take a deep breath and listen to the horse's breathing as you watch his or her stomach rise and fall with each breath taken. Allow your breath to synchronize with the horse's. If you're close to the horse's head, feel his or her breath on your skin, feeling the warmth of each breath as the horse exhales. Again notice whatever you are feeling, just observing any emotions as they arise.

Now bring your attention to the earth beneath your feet, feeling its support beneath you, noticing how much earth there is. Begin to notice it is the same earth as the horse is standing on. Feel the earth that you share together.

This is your time to share whatever you need to with this loving animal. It is your time together. Be open to receiving, for the horse, too, has much to offer.

It is time now to thank this magnificent animal for the time you have shared together. Take this time now to thank your horse for the gifts and time you have shared, knowing that you get to bring this presence with you, as you begin to slowly bring your presence back to the room. Feel the support of the chair or the floor beneath you, notice any sounds that are present, and allow your breathing to return to normal. Slowly begin to move your body, wiggle your fingers and your toes, stretch, and move your body, and when you're ready, open your eyes, bringing yourself fully into the present moment.

Meditation

Meditation is another valuable tool in achieving harmony both with horses and with ourselves. Meditation can be defined as the focusing of attention inwardly, usually to a single point of reference, on a thought or awareness. As with visualization, meditation can create neurological patterns that then lead to muscular response. By the inward focus of our attention on a specific thought and body response, we can increase our bodies' ability to act and respond in this manner. For example, spending ten minutes a few times a week focusing on the sensation of our breath entering and exiting our bodies, and catching our thoughts wandering and then returning them to our breathing, can increase the relaxation response in our bodies every time we take a deep breath.

Another benefit of the inward focus of our attention through meditation is the increased connectedness with our true selves. Many of us lead busy lives and rarely have time for ourselves. By creating some time to spend with ourselves, we can let go of the expectations of others and get back in touch with our own desires. Horses often create this time for us. Have you ever had the experience of being at the barn when no one is around but you and your horse? Can you remember how your stresses slowly drifted away and you began to feel calm, content, and clear? This in itself is a form of active meditation.

There are many types of meditation and many ways we can use it to enhance our work with horses. Meditation can help us improve our ability to control the activation levels in our nervous systems, improve our visualization skills, focus our breathing, connect with our intuition, and promote relaxation and positive intention.

Chapter 9: Intuition

Listening to Intuition

Have you ever had a thought and acted on it not knowing why, only to later realize how important your action or thought was? It's commonly referred to as a gut feeling or intuition. Intuition essentially is the knowing of something without prior knowledge or the use of reason. It's a thought that comes to us and guides us in the right direction if we listen.

We all have experienced intuition at some point or another in our lives, even if it's to say, "My gut told me, but I listened to my brain instead." For me, intuition plays a big role in my work with horses. After numerous experiences of finding myself on the ground, brushing dirt off of myself while wondering why I had not listened to that insistent thought that questioned if I was doing the right thing, I decided to start listening to my intuition.

For me, listening to my intuition often means working outside the box, doing things that don't necessarily make sense in my rational thought process. Sometimes it's as simple as going back a few lessons on a youngster I'm starting, or other times it's working a horse in a way that initially doesn't seem to coincide with the overall object-ive of the behavior consult. What I have found is there is always a higher reason for the intuition, and the more I listen to my intuition, the more it speaks to me. The more it speaks to me, the easier it gets to recognize it as intuition rather than fear or expectations.

A Lesson in Trusting My Intuition

I was preparing to mount a beautiful warmblood filly that I was starting. I had already sat on her a handful of times and even walked around on her. She had graduated to me getting straight into the saddle, rather than bellying over her back first, a few days earlier. I listened as the thought came to my head that I should belly over and have her owner lead us in a small circle before I got on. As I explained to the owner what I wanted her to do, she asked if the filly was showing me any signs that influenced my decision. My answer was no, nothing in particular. I was simply listening to my intuition.

The owner led the filly forward once I was bel-lied over the saddle. After only a couple of steps, the filly let out a few bucks, and I pushed myself off to safety as the owner stopped the filly. We then started over. This time the filly relaxed, and soon I was riding her around at the walk. I am still not exactly sure why the filly bucked, but I am glad I listened to my intuition and created a safe, positive session for everyone involved.

Chapter 10: Self-Awareness

Horses and Self-Awareness

Horses are often our greatest teachers. They recognize us for our truest selves and respond to us accordingly. They react and interact with us according to our emotions and the universal language of energy. They respond to who we are and are not fooled by who we pretend to be. I believe this is why so many of us feel so close to these incredible animals and feel free when we are with them. They allow us to be ourselves, and even more, they accept us as we are.

Self-awareness is a great asset when working with horses. Whether or not you recognize your true feelings in a situation, your horse will respond accordingly. By just being aware of how you are feeling, you can start to make changes. We all lack confidence, experience uncertainty, and even feel scared or nervous at times. By acknowledging your feelings, even if it is only to yourself, you can easily gain confidence by using tools such as breathing, singing, and positive thinking.

IF YOUR HORSE COULD TALK

Your horse will sense even the slightest shift in your emotions and adjust accordingly.

Furthermore, by acknowledging how you are feeling rather than what you think you should be feeling, you enable change. Sometimes the change will come quickly. Just by being honest about how you are feeling, your emotions will start to shift. Other times the movement will be gradual. You will recognize where you are in that moment and where you would like to be. These two pieces of information will help you discover what tools can assist you in achieving your goal. Either way, by accepting your real feelings, you give yourself the power to change.

A Lesson in Self-Awareness

Breeze consistently challenged me to be authentic and congruent. With her it was never a sometimes gig. This is probably why I found so many ups and downs in my relationship with Breeze, why at some times I was so uncomfortable in it and others so fulfilled. One of the many gifts Breeze shared with me was forcing me to be present when I rode.

Starting my riding career as a scared kid, and then continuing it in an industry that taught me to ignore and push through my fear, had caused me to create a false persona of toughness when I rode. For the most part, I was able to push through any fear and ride horses that many others wouldn't. In fact, at the time I probably would have told you I had no fear in the saddle. Breeze broke through that façade quickly.

Breeze had her own fears, issues, and trauma when it came to being ridden. Our first couple of months together were focused on teaching her to walk under saddle. Her nervousness caused her to trot and prance everywhere. Once she could walk under saddle with a contact, it was a whole new lesson for her to walk on a long rein when no one was holding her back. She was quick to react and hard to settle. Breeze was just a scared and confused pony looking for direction. When she did react, she quickly looked to me for that direction, but not from my aids. The aids actually caused her more stress. She responded mostly to interspecies communication, to how I was feeling and what messages my mind and body were sharing with her.

I had spent all these years burying my fears, riding horses others wouldn't, and now a fourteen-hand pony was stripping away my walls and seeing me for who I really was, a scared and insecure rider. As situations from my past seemed to replay themselves, like bolting across the ring as I had with Willie, I became aware that I was very much a part of these situations. I became aware that I was scared, that when Breeze needed security from me the most, I was insecure. This was a very hard pill to swallow, but there was no avoiding it. Trust me. I tried.

Recognizing that I did have fear started me on the path I am on today. For me, it did not disappear from my experiences with Breeze. The experiences just allowed me to find a way forward, to experience my fear, and to learn ways to help me through it. Without Breeze, I'm not sure I would have explored all the topics I am sharing with you in this book. At times her ability to see the real me was scary, but in the end, we faced our fears together, and I know I am a better rider, trainer, teacher, and person because of it.

Congruency

Horses are naturally intuitive and self-aware animals. It is as if they have X-ray goggles that strip away all the ideals and images that we present as ourselves and see only the true essence of who we are. In today's society, it is easy to get caught up in materialism and society's ideals of who we should be. In doing this, we spend so much time trying to be who others think we should be that we lose awareness of who we really are. We begin to see ourselves as the image we project rather than our true selves. If we are communicating from the perspective of who we think we should be, and our horses are communicating with us for who we are, the chance of miscommunication increases.

Here is a diagram to help you understand how self-awareness will improve your relationship with your horse. It is used with the permission of Context International.

The circle on the left represents the image we present to the world. This is where we as humans tend to function and communicate. It is made up of all our beliefs around who we think we should be, who we would like to be, and who we think we are. This is the person we create in our minds.

The circle on the right represents who we really are. This is where horses communicate from. The circle on the right is where we are in our purest form, when we are honest with ourselves. If we are truthful with ourselves and aware of our thoughts, our bodies, and our emotions, we bring our circles closer together. This place of overlap, this place of congruency, is where we communicate with horses. So the more in touch with our true selves we become, the clearer our communications with others, both horse and human, will be.

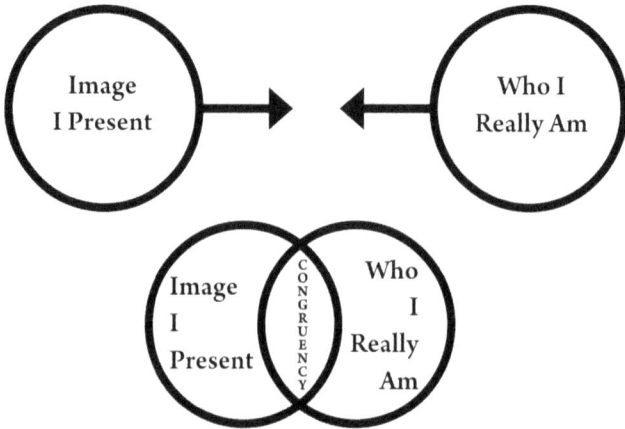

Image I Present- Where humans tend to communicate from.
Who I Really Am- Where horses communicate from.
Congruency- Where we can most effectively communicate with horses from.

Self-Awareness and Communication

Communication is a meeting place where two beings come together to share thoughts and perceptions with each other. For both parties to arrive at the same place, they must not only know where they are meeting, but they also must know where they are in the moment. Think of it like a GPS. You can know where you want to go and have every intention of getting there, but if you cannot enter your starting location, you cannot get directions. Furthermore, if you enter a starting location other than your current location, the directions are going to get you even more lost.

Exercise 6: Horse Lover's GPS

Finding Your Starting Location

Now it's time to find our true starting location. This takes honesty. Sometimes being truthful with ourselves can be frightening. Remember, your horse already sees you and appreciates you for who you really are, and right now you just have to be truthful with yourself. Here are some questions you can ask yourself. Take time and be truthful. Taking a few moments to do a body scan before you start this exercise is a great idea.

1. How do I feel right now? (It's okay if the answer is angry or scared.)
2. What do I think I should feel right now?
3. Why do I think I should feel this way?
4. How would I like to be feeling right now? (This is how you would like to feel, not how you think others expect you to feel.)

Now complete the following sentence. This sentence will be your starting place.

In this moment, being honest with myself, I feel ....

Finding Your Destination

Now that you have successfully pinpointed your starting location, it is time to choose your destination. Your destination is a meeting place for you and your horse. This means deciding on a location that benefits both of you, most often on neutral ground. Again honesty is important. You may want to look over "Goal Setting" on page 174 before completing this exercise. Here are some questions to ask yourself.

1. How would I like to feel right now?
2. Why would I like to feel this way?
3. How does my feeling this way benefit my horse?
4. Will this help create neutrality in my communications?

Now complete the following sentence. This is your destination.

I would like to feel .... right now. I honestly believe feeling .... is in the best interest of both me and my horse.

The Journey

Now that you know where you are and where you are going, take some time to decide on a route. There are always many ways to reach a destination. Choose one that meets the needs of you and your horse. This book will give you a wide variety of tools to help you on your journey. It is normal to try a few options before you find the right one. Focus on your destination, and if you feel lost or off track, ask yourself: how do I really feel right now? This will help you course correct and get back on track. Remember the journey is as important as the destination.

Who I Am versus What I Do

As I started on a journey to learn more about myself and the joy that horses bring to me, I began to realize how much of "who I am" is tied up in being a horse person. I also realized how often being a "horse person" causes me to put judgments and expectations on myself that actually disconnect me from horses and the joy they bring me. The concept of ego or false self, a concept that is unique to the human species, is extremely relevant in working with horses.

Understanding my false self is priceless in my work with horses as well as in every other area of my life. I have taken numerous seminars and courses that discussed the topic of false self, also referred to as the image I present to the world. I was able to recognize many aspects of my false self personas as well as understand how "what I do" is often wrongly identified as "who I am." While I understood the concept of mistaking "what I do" for "who I am," it wasn't until I attended my first Epona Approach workshop that I gained a deeper understanding of how it related to me.

Epona Approach workshops are self-development workshops for horse people and non-horse people alike. Horses are present in the capacity of teachers, nothing more. As I interacted in an environment that forced me to step out of "horse trainer" mode and into just being with horses, my false self persona of "horse trainer" became very apparent. I realized how much I identified being a horse trainer with who I was. I also recognized that the majority of the time that I encountered major resistance from a horse or when things went "badly," I was getting concerned with what people would think of me as a "trainer." As I aligned with my false self and became caught up in the image I was presenting to others, I became incongruent. This left little clear ground for the horse to communicate with me on. Just by being aware of my "horse trainer" false self, I am able to catch myself slipping into it much sooner and bring my focus back to the present moment.

Mirror, Mirror in the Stall

I believe that we attract people and animals into our lives. Furthermore, the people and the animals in our lives mirror us. They share with us a reflection of ourselves. Sometimes we like what we see and sometimes we do not. I have found this to be especially true through my personal experiences with horses as well as helping clients and their horses work through issues that arise. Because horses communicate with us on the basis of who we really are, the learning they have to offer us about ourselves is incredible.

Looking back, I can laugh at all the times I felt so angry and frustrated and lost with Breeze, as I now recognize I was feeling lost and angry and frustrated with myself. Even now I have "aha" moments as I discover a piece of myself and recognize it in the mirrors Breeze shared with me.

When Breeze arrived in my life, she was a contradictory balance of fear of being alone, and anger when someone looked at her too closely or tried to be physically close to her. She would panic, running and screaming, if she was separated from her friends. She would make very threatening faces as I brought people to see my new pony. When I touched her, especially in her more vulnerable areas, she would threaten and fidget, now and then even giving a small kick. She was me through and through.

I have always had a deep need for connecting with people yet a huge fear of being vulnerable. It has been very challenging meeting that need for connection when I put up walls, most often through anger and aggression, whenever anyone tried to know me. In my younger years, drinking seemed like a great way to connect with others because I would let my guard down and relax. Unfortunately, all the self-destructive behavior that went along with drinking only reinforced my dislike for me and my resolve that it was better to keep people from really knowing me.

I think I am so drawn to horses because they see the real me despite how hard I may try at times to shut others out. Breeze was such a gift in my life because to help her move through her attitude, I had to move through my own. It was only when I was being open and authentic that she felt safe with me and shared with me her true self. Our bond grew stronger and stronger, and it was with her I shared some of the most raw and intimate pieces of myself. At the same time, the moment I got stuck in my stuff, she gave it right back to me. I believe we taught each other the joy that comes from letting our guard down and showing up as who we really are.

Receiving Interspecies Communications

As well as having the ability to share our emotions, thoughts, and feelings with others through the language of energy, we can also receive others' thought, feeling, and emotional vibrations. People tend to think of those who are able to receive these vibrations from animals as rare and uniquely gifted people. While these animal communicators or animal whisperers usually are unique and gifted individuals, we are all able to receive these communications.

The reason most people are unaware of their ability to receive vibrational communications is that they are not aware of where they are truly at. To be clearly aware of another being's vibrations or energy, we must be conscious and in alignment with our own. We spend our lives being told by our parents, teachers, friends, religious leaders, and politicians who and what we need to be. Somehow who we are becomes not enough or not "right." We start to bury our unique thoughts and emotions and put on a happy face or tough face or whatever face we think we should present to the world. In doing this, the image of who we present to the world becomes separated from who we really are. Amazingly enough, we start to believe the image we create, and we interact with the world and with ourselves from this place.

By being honest with ourselves about how we are truly feeling at the moment, we can start to recognize what that emotion feels like within our minds and bodies. The more awareness we bring to what we are feeling, the more we are aware of where we are truly at, without the influence of someone else's thoughts and opinions. As we gain clarity in what thoughts and emotions are our own, we will also gain clarity as to when another being's energy or vibration is affecting us. Like a radio, we cannot expect to receive a certain station until we are able to tune in to that frequency.

Again I refer to the diagram on page 76. Horses communicate from the circle on the right, which represents our true selves. For us to receive a vibrational communication from the horse, we must be in tune or in alignment with our true selves. The more congruent we are with our true selves, the clearer we will receive as well as send communications.

Chapter 11: Emotions

Anger and Horses

Getting angry and losing our temper is common among horse lovers. More often than not, it doesn't resolve the issue at hand, and if it does, it's usually only a temporary fix. We end up leaving the barn feeling upset and guilty and find ourselves far from a place of harmony, either with ourselves or our horses. If this experience sounds familiar to you, the good news is that you're human and you are likely reading this book looking for a better way. The even better news is that by recognizing your anger and understanding why you get angry, you are allowing yourself the opportunity to grow.

Two common reasons for a person to get angry are fear and frustration. Horses are large animals whose brains and instincts function very differently from ours. No wonder we sometimes hit a place of fear and/or frustration!

Fear

A normal response when an animal feels threatened is to fight. This is also true of humans. Working with horses can be intimidating enough when they behave, but when they start to test us, invade our personal boundaries, or go into instinct mode, it can be overwhelming. To make matters worse, if we don't understand why they are acting the way they are, our fears may escalate. By learning what a horse's natural instincts are, the psychology of a horse, how to safely establish boundaries, equine body language, and how our energy and emotions affect the horse, we increase our understanding of horses and lessen our fears. By reducing our fears and using the tools in this chapter to work through them, we are less likely to become angry, and when we do, we will have more tools to work through the issue at hand.

Frustration

Anger and frustration are closely linked. Often when we hit the wall of frustration, our tempers take over. Frustration arises when we cannot find a solution and when we feel at a loss for an answer, which leads to feeling helpless. Luckily, every problem has a solution. By remaining open and thinking outside of the box, we can find the solution. Ask for help; there may be someone who already has a solution or can offer a different perspective. Try again tomorrow. Sometimes calming down and sleeping on it will bring us more ideas.

Another factor that I find essential in keeping my cool and not allowing fear and frustration to take over is focusing on where both the horse and I are at in the present moment. Often if we become too focused on where we want to be, we lose sight of where we are. We start to worry about all the "what ifs" instead of what is. When you feel anger coming up, take a moment to assess where both you and the horse are right now and work forward from there.

A Lesson in Anger

I grew up a very angry and unhappy teenager. Looking back, I realize how much of my anger came from my confusion and frustration in not knowing how to deal with my naturally sensitive nature when it came to other people's energy. I couldn't separate the vibrations I picked up from others from my own and often felt overwhelmed, alone, and scared. I had a short temper and was often overtaken with anger.

At age sixteen, a horse named Jolly Olly came into my life. After several very successful years of showing with my horse Pacific Shadow, my parents bought me Olly to take me to the next level. That he did, but not in the show ring as I expected. Olly was a very successful jumper whose whole life had been spent as a show horse. As I taught him how to let down and enjoy being a best friend, he taught me how a best friend should and should not behave.

One of the first things Olly felt I should learn was that taking my temper and anger out on

IF YOUR HORSE COULD TALK

another was not appropriate. Olly's show horse background had made him familiar with artificial aids such as whips and spurs. When I used these pieces of equipment to support my natural aids, such as hand, leg, and seat, and my intentions were pure, Olly had no problem responding nicely. Yet when I used any aids, including natural ones, from a place of anger, Olly would promptly stop and rear or buck on the spot until I dealt with my anger.

I quickly learned to check my mood before and throughout my time with Olly and only did things that allowed me to feel more positive. Some days this meant just grooming or lunging. Other days, as I took my time just being with him, with no expectations, my mood would shift, and I would eventually get on and ride. Dealing fully with my anger was a long process, but Olly started off by teaching me to recognize my anger, and through an awareness of it came the possibility for my mood to shift.

The Gift of Fear

Many of you are probably familiar with the saying "Cowboy Up." For those of you who are not, it means to persevere in times of adversity. As humans, we are often taught to override our emotions and toughen up. I find this especially true in the horse world as we are often taught we have to be tougher and more aggressive than our horses to be in control. This means pushing fear aside and getting on with it. Fear is an emotion many of us feel ashamed of and do not even like to admit to ourselves.

Horses have a very different viewpoint on fear than humans do. For horses, fear is not a negative emotion to cast aside. It is a gift to embrace as fear signals to them that their survival may be at risk. It allows them to respond accordingly and then get on with life. When a horse is left to his own devices, he will respond to whatever he fears in a manner he feels appropriate. He will then move on. This may mean exploring his curiosity from a safer distance and approaching what he initially feared as he gains confidence about his safety, or it may simply mean he feels safe where he is and the experience is over. Either way because he has embraced his fear, he has released it.

Have you ever noticed when you are scared of something but always push the fear aside, your anticipation of it actually seems to grow? If we never embrace our fears, we do not allow ourselves to move forward through them. Fear has a gift to share with us if we are willing to accept it. If we can acknowledge our fear, it will guide us forward. It is there for a reason.

By embracing your fear, you open yourself up to the lesson it has to share. Fear will keep you safe if you accept it. To ignore it could actually put you in harm's way. It can keep you safe because it will tell you when to be cautious. If you ignore your fear and enter into a situation you are uncertain about, you are not only entering a potentially dangerous situation, but you are also doing so in fear, whether you admit it or not. Have you ever noticed how quickly fear spreads among both horses and humans? Have you ever noticed how nervous horses become around nervous people?

By accepting our fear, we can then put ourselves in a place where we feel safe. From this place of safety, we can explore the situation and find ways to move forward that do feel safe. For example, I am asked to ride a young horse that is very tense and anxious, and I notice I am feeling fearful. I could push my fear aside and get on anyway. The youngster would feel my fear, I would feel his anxiety, and we would feed off each other, escalating our emotions. I would have increased the level of danger in this situation.

My other option is to embrace my fear. I acknowledge it and look for something to do with the youngster that I feel comfortable with. I go over and pet him. He notices I am calm and starts to relax a little. I feel much better than I did when I thought of riding him. I feel safe leading him around the ring. I notice he has some excess energy that he is holding onto. I feel good about lunging him. I think of what exercises I would feel comfortable doing with him on the lunge. Transitions sound good. On the lunge line, he starts to pick up on my calm demeanor. By focusing on transitions, he starts to concentrate, and he gets his excess energy out. By the time I'm done lunging, I feel ready to get on.

This is a great example of how listening to my fear can guide me to a better situation for both me and the horse. Sometimes moving through your fear may be a much longer process. It may include furthering your education, gaining your confidence on a quieter horse, or even seeking the help of someone more experienced. Accepting fear does not mean never pushing your comfort zone; it just means recognizing it and finding a way to move forward from a place where you feel more positive about the situation than negative.

There may also be situations where a fear overwhelms you. In situations like these, I recommend considering if there is trauma involved. For more information on this, review the section on trauma on page 205.

Exercise 7: Fear's Message

Through my work with Deborah Marshall and studies of Linda Kohanov's "Emotional Message Chart," I have learned the importance of listening to fear's message. Here are some questions to ask yourself as soon as you feel fear. It is important to feel the fear and ask the questions rather than pushing it aside.
What is the threat?

Am I in real danger in this moment?

If the answer is yes, what must I do to move to a position of safety?

If the answer is no, what danger am I anticipating? What other options do I have, and what option feels better?

Part 3: Horse Psychology

Bravo and I enjoying a ride together. Photo courtesy of Leigh Smith.

Chapter 12: Understanding Horse Psychology

From the Horse's Perspective

Understanding where our horses are coming from is an essential part of creating successful relationships with them. By learning how our horses think, learn, and process information as well as understanding their natural instincts, we increase the size of our toolbox immensely. Horses, like humans, are all individual and learn and react in their own unique way. All too often when we run into problems with one horse, we try and solve it the same way we did with another horse. What works with one horse will not necessarily work with another, and even more importantly, what worked in one situation with one horse will not work in another situation with the same horse.

Learning to look at circumstances from a horse's perspective will increase our ability to understand and communicate with horses. All too often, issues that arise in relationships between horses and humans are simply a matter of miscommunication. Being on the same page is an essential part of communication.

Educating ourselves on the psychology of the horse enables us to treat each situation creatively and with an open mind. This open mind in turn offers us many options and solutions so we can choose what will work best for the individuality of each horse.

Bravo: The Importance of Understanding Horse Psychology

In my work, I am often called as a last resort, when the horse is scared, angry, or traumatized. I often see horses screaming for help, and the owners are unaware or unwilling to ask for or receive help. Yet sometimes people come along and restore my faith. My client Leigh is one of those people. She contacted me one summer to help her start her three-year-old Quarter Horse, Bravo. He was a large, handsome, chestnut gelding with a personality that could not be missed.

Leigh had not been planning on buying a young horse, but the mare she bought turned out to have career-ending soundness issues. The breeder, in admirable integrity (again restoring my faith), took the mare back and gave her Bravo instead. Before I met Bravo, he had a handful of rides but was still very much a baby as training goes. Leigh had a natural horsemanship trainer out before me. She chose to end this after one session when she saw how obviously stressed and upset Bravo was.

This is one of the reasons I admire Leigh. Although she had a young horse she desperately wanted started and did not know of any other options at the time, she chose to put Bravo's well-being first. My understanding is even at the time I met Leigh, she was seriously considering selling Bravo. She needed a safe and reliable horse that she could enjoy riding. Whether or not this young, dominant horse would fit this description was still in question.

I quickly realized Bravo was a strong-willed, dominant, highly intelligent youngster with lots of spunk. Leigh had been lunging Bravo regularly, but he thought it was just an excuse to buck and play. In the beginning, Bravo was definitely one of those horses that was not impressed with the new girl. He was very full of himself and was not going to be told what to do. While he didn't out-right misbehave when we worked him, he did not want to be caught and would threaten me with flattened ears when I came near. There were a number of sessions in the beginning that he did not make it out of his paddock as I worked to establish leadership in his home, with him loose. Being the smart guy that he was, he tried every trick that he could think of before considering working with me. I believe there are true pivotal points in a young horse's life. These sessions in the paddock were that for Bravo.

By the time we made it back to the ring, Bravo progressed at an incredible rate. All the energy

IF YOUR HORSE COULD TALK

he had previously put into trying to outsmart me was now channelled into trying to please me. I often had to slow things down because he was so smart and tried so hard to do the right thing that he would become anxious anticipating what I wanted. During this time, Leigh was there for every session, asking questions and stepping in to lunge and later ride as soon as both she and Bravo were ready. By the end of the summer, we were hauling Bravo, with a companion, over to another barn for some basic dressage lessons.

Leigh decided to keep Bravo as he proved that when his strong personality was focused in the right direction, he was more than suitable. He still has lots of excess energy when he has time off, but he makes it clear on the ground when he needs lunging before being ridden. One of the things I enjoy most about Bravo is his ability to work with you or against you. He is a horse that demands to be ridden softly. The more strength the rider uses, the more strength he responds with. This can be frustrating at times, yet he safely challenges his riders to be their best, to be assertive without becoming aggressive. Working with Leigh and Bravo was truly refreshing for me as I realized that Bravo is a horse that I want working for me, not against me. Leigh's willingness to find a trainer she felt comfortable with, and to then dedicate herself fully to the starting process, made all this possible for Bravo. He is a very lucky horse.

Chapter 13:
Horses as a Species

The Importance of Understanding Horses as a Species

Horses and humans have come together to create partnerships for many centuries. This partnership includes both predator and prey. In general, most domestic horses adapt to the human lifestyle and function well within our "herd." If we mirror the willingness of the horses to adapt, and start to interact with them in a way that is more natural to them, imagine what we can achieve. By recognizing the differences between horses and humans, we can often find simple solutions to problems. To learn to think like horses, we must look at their natural lifestyle and the innate behaviors crucial to their survival. The following are some ideas to think about when working with your horse.

Horses Are Herd Animals

In the wild, horses live in family groups called herds. The herd protects and watches out for each other. Each horse has a different role within the herd. This role reflects his or her individual strengths and weaknesses. A lead mare, called the matriarch mare, runs the herd. She is the one to make the decisions as to the herd's survival. This includes letting others know if their behavior, within the herd, is acceptable or not. The stallion is the protector of the herd. He works alongside the lead mare to ensure the herd's safety and survival.

Horses look to their leaders for information and direction. In the wild, a solitary horse is not likely to survive because predators are more likely to prey on him. When a horse is behaving in a way that is detrimental to the well-being of the herd, the lead mare will send the horse to the outskirts of the herd. Being sent away from the herd is the worst punishment a horse can receive.

A Lesson in Herd Dynamics

I have been aware for quite some time that horses can accept humans into their herd, and I have often been welcomed into a herd. The summer I spent starting Bravo gave me a whole new perspective of being in a herd. When I entered into Bravo's herd, he was king of the farm. He was dominant over Leigh and her other horse, and he was convinced he would be over me also. That was why so many sessions were spent in his paddock in the beginning. It was also why he started to threaten me with his ears and body language. I challenged his dominance and asked to be the leader.

This was necessary. If we had been hanging out in a large pasture and I had been learning how to live in the horse world, it would have made sense for him to call the shots. But we were working in the human world, training him to become a dressage horse. My leadership was necessary. He accepted my new position and allowed me to lead. Leigh also allowed me to do this, trusting my knowledge of starting young horses.

When Leigh started working with Bravo, I was there helping her. Many of my methods were new to both her and Bravo, and it made sense that I would guide them both. During this time, Bravo did little to challenge Leigh when she asked him to do things. The time came when we all felt ready for them to do some work on their own.

The first time I came out after they had worked on their own, I asked Leigh how it had gone. She described to me how he had challenged her leadership in ways that he hadn't previously. She had remembered how I had dealt with his challenging behavior in the beginning and responded to him accordingly. They worked through things, and Bravo soon recognized her leadership skills whether I was there or not. Many people would have seen Bravo's behavior as bad and wrong. In terms of the nature of the horse, Bravo saw my absence as lack of leadership and stepped

IF YOUR HORSE COULD TALK

up to fill the void. When Leigh also stepped up, Bravo challenged her to make sure she truly was the best leader for their survival. When he realized she was, he backed down and allowed her to lead. To me, this situation was actually a great gift because Leigh and Bravo evolved into their own herd.

This is also a great example of why a trainer can never "fix" your horse for you. It is common for horses to be sent away for training and when they return home slide back into old behaviors. The assistance of a trainer is often needed to start a young horse or when problems arise, but the owner/rider's involvement is necessary for true growth. If Leigh had not been so involved in the beginning when I did most of the work with Bravo, she may not have known how to handle the situation, and it would likely have escalated.

Survival Instincts

While it helps to recognize that horses are prey animals, it is even more important to understand what that means in terms of survival instincts. Knowing what your horse's instinctual response is will better equip you to help him adjust to the human world.

- Horses are herbivores. This means they do not eat meat or hunt other animals. Horses graze for vegetation and, unlike predators, they do not instinctively relate actions to food rewards. Excessive energy outbursts actually mean less time for eating and more energy needed from food, which can cause trouble in the wild. The digestive system of a horse functions best when fed a little on a continuous basis. Therefore horses are energy preservers in order to survive.

- Horses are into pressure animals, meaning if you push on them they will push back. This is likely due to the fact that when attacked by a wild cat or a wild dog, the horse's best chance of survival is to lean into the teeth, and when the predator goes to regrip, the horse can pull away without his intestines being ripped out. It is due to us that domestic horses learn to move away from pressure. Horses that pull back when tied, run through the bridle, and move into leg pressure are all examples of horses that are moving into pressure.

- Horses are distractible. They have a large area of awareness and keep shifting their focus as new stimuli occur. They rely on their senses to constantly update them on their surroundings. Focusing on one thing for a long period of time leaves a horse vulnerable to predators. It is common to see a horse standing guard as another sleeps, eats, drinks, or relaxes. This is another way horses use the herd to their advantage. In the human world, when a horse trusts a human to look out for his well-being, he will have an easier time focusing on work and what is being asked of him.

Senses of the Horse

Our senses enable us to perceive the world around us and give us important information in a variety of ways. Horses' senses do the same for them. As predators by nature, our senses differ in some ways from those of horses, who are prey animals. Below is a list of some of these differences.

- Horses' brains work differently than ours. The left side of a horse's brain controls the left side of his body, and the right side of his brain controls the right side of his body. Roughly 20 percent of the information transfers from one side of a horse's brain to the other. Therefore showing horses things from both sides is helpful.
- Horses see 340 degrees around them. They have binocular vision in front and monocular vision on each side. They have a blind spot directly behind them and another up to six feet in front of them. They must lower their heads to see in this area.
- A horse's lens has little adjustability, so he is sensitive to sudden light changes and must move his head to focus. Spooking is

actually a horse adjusting his body so he is able to quickly focus on an object and take a better look. Horses are able to notice very subtle movements.

- Horses have 180 degrees mobility in each ear and move the ear to the direction information is coming from. Horses detect a greater range of sound than humans, at both higher and lower frequencies.

Flight, Fight, Freeze, and Deep Freeze

Horses are flight animals. When put in a dangerous situation, they will exercise the option to run, fight, or freeze. Flight, fight, and freeze are responses of high activation in the nervous system. Flight is generally the first response, with fight most often being used when all options of flight are taken away. A horse tends to run one-quarter to three-eighths of a mile before he will even think to stop and look behind him. A horse usually exercises every option of flight, trying all six directions: forward, back, right, left, up, and down. When a horse believes he is helpless and is unsure how to escape the situation, he will freeze. Although he is immobile, the nervous system may still be in high activation, assessing options and possible danger. Deep freeze is essentially when an animal gives up. The body physically responds, shutting down the nervous system and entering a painless state.

Adrenaline is one of the hormones released in the body when an animal is put in a flight or fight situation. When an animal or human is in physical or emotional distress, adrenaline is secreted, and the sympathetic nervous system responds. The heart and respiration rate will increase, the blood flow to the muscles will increase, and alertness will increase. The horse's reaction time will become more rapid, and the immune and digestive systems will start to slow down. The slowing down of the digestive system allows the blood supply to flow to the limbs and organs necessary for immediate survival.

Although some activation in the nervous system will help achieve tasks, too much activation shuts down the horse's ability to think. In this state of high activation, the horse goes into survival mode, responding instinctively and no longer learning.

It is important to remember that much of what we ask horses to participate in, in our human world, goes against their survival instincts. This means things that we see as part of life may cause horses stress. More importantly, if horses reach a state of high activation, the likelihood of them learning and processing information in this state is extremely low. If we continue to apply pressure when they are in this heightened state of awareness, we confirm their belief that this is a potentially dangerous situation.

For example, horses are herd animals and rely on the security of their herd for survival in the wild.

In the domesticated world, horses are expected to be able to focus on their rider/handler, whether other horses are around or not. For some horses, going against their natural instincts and ignoring the presence or absence of another horse is very stressful. The more stress horses experience, the more their instincts take over, causing them to focus even more on their friends. This is most often accompanied by a rise in adrenaline and loss in the level of learning.

When I start young horses, I keep the first few lessons simple and low key. This allows the young-sters to find success even if they are distracted being away from their friends. It also creates positive sessions away from their friends, which give them confidence in the horse/human herd.

Understanding How Horses Learn

By understanding how horses learn, we can be better equipped to find harmonious solutions as well as to understand why a horse is acting a certain way. Below is a list of ways horses learn and an example of each type of learning. Take some time to consider a recent training situation with your horse and identify what type or types of learning were taking place.

- Horses learn by association. This means relating objects and experiences to each other. It refers to learning that two different events or experiences occur or happen together. *Shadow was my childhood jumper. We both liked to go fast, and we both liked to win. In a jumper class, the whistle will blow to signal that the timers are ready. If you manage to jump the first round clear, you usually stay in the ring for the jump-off, which is all about speed. The whistle will blow again to tell you the timers are ready. In his many years as a show horse, Shadow had learned to associate the whistle with going fast, especially when he got to stay in the ring and hear it a second time. I had to be ready for that second whistle because once Shadow heard it he was going, with or without my asking.*

- Horses learn by classical conditioning. This is learning through establishing association between different events and stimuli. It involves pairing a neutral stimulus with an unconditioned one to create a desired response. *When I am starting a horse, I use classical conditioning to teach the horse to respond to voice commands, the lunge line, and the long lines/bit. My body language is an unconditioned stimulus that directs the horse's speed and direction. I can condition the horse to react to voice commands, the lunge line, or long lines, which are all neutral stimuli, by simultaneously using them with my body language.*

- Horses learn by habituation. This means getting used to things. By repeated exposure to something, a decrease in responsiveness usually occurs. *A young horse is nervous about having his blanket put on. Every night his owner calmly and patiently puts the blanket on. After a week, the young horse is much more relaxed and accepting of the blanket. By the end of the month, he doesn't seem to even notice the blanket going on.*

- Horses learn by positive reinforcement. This is when the use of stimulus with a positive reward creates an increase in the frequency of a particular behavior. *Thomas is unsure of the blue tarp by the hay shed. Every time he is brave and takes a step toward it, his owner gives him a big pet and tells him how smart he is. Thomas loves attention from his owner. Pretty soon he realizes the tarp isn't hurting him and he gets lots of attention when he walks toward it. Before long, Thomas heads toward the tarp every time he sees it.*

- Horses learn by negative reinforcement. This is when the frequency of a behavior is increased with the removal of an unpleasant stimulus. *A trainer is riding a youngster who is just being started. The trainer practices halt transitions by softly pulling on the reins and saying "ho." The youngster dislikes the bit and at first opens her mouth in resistance. When this doesn't make a difference to the contact on her mouth, she halts. The trainer immediately releases the pressure on the bit. After a few repetitions, the youngster quickly catches on that if she halts when pressure is applied to the bit, the pressure goes away.*

- Horses are latent learners. They learn and process information that you do not see them learning at the time. At a later date when there is some reinforcement or incentive to demonstrate the learning, you will see it. It's as if they learned it overnight. *My horse Isabella had spent most of her young life out in a pasture with other horses and was not very familiar with the human world. A few days a week, I take her for a walk around the farm where I keep her. The first day I took her out, there was a horse blanket on the fence. She was terrified. I gave her plenty of time to walk by it, and when she finally did, she scooted by, giving it a wide berth. The next time I took her out, she walked by it without stopping or spooking. Although I had not seen her learning the first day, she had learned that the blanket was not a threat.*

- Horses think in pictures. They see a slide show of associated pictures. *When Moon was a young horse, a plastic bag blew through his paddock and wrapped around his leg. He became frightened and ran off. When Classy was a young horse, her owner brought her apples in a noisy, white plastic bag. Moon's strongest memory of a plastic bag is being "attacked" by one, and every time he sees a plastic bag, his mind starts a slide show of the bag coming at him and him running away. This slide show will continue unless someone takes the time to strengthen a different memory of a plastic bag. Classy's strongest memory of a plastic bag is being brought apples. Every time she sees or hears a plastic bag, a slide show of her being fed apples runs through her mind, and she approaches, searching for the treat.*

- Horses learn when the activation level of their nervous system is regulated. They have to be calm enough to give their attention in order to learn. *When I first got Breeze, she was very nervous and wild on the lunge line. Her experiences thus far had been galloping around, scared and out of control. As soon as I sent her out on the circle on a lunge line, she would enter a state of high activation and would act as if I no longer existed. I started ground driving her with two lines and realized she was much more relaxed. After a ground driving session, I would end by cooling her out at the walk on the lunge line. At this time, she had already worked out her excess energy and was much more relaxed with the activation level in her nervous system down. Over time, I decreased the amount of work I did ground driving her and increased the work on the lunge line, as long as her activation level stayed within range. Over time, Breeze learned to stay focused and calm on the lunge because with her nervous system regulated she was able to learn what I was asking of her.*

- Horses are natural mimics and learn by following another horse's actions. This learning comes from doing the action and following the other horse's lead rather than watching the action. *I introduced Apollo to the river as a yearling. He was very suspicious and cautious of the slow-moving water. At first he was not at all interested in crossing the river. His friend Zena crossed it ahead of him, but he was still uncertain. I decided to keep my feet dry by hopping over the river via a few well-placed rocks. Watching me now cross after already watching Zena, Apollo decided to mimic me. Unfortunately, his large feet were too big for the rocks, and he had trouble following my route. He kept trying, certain that it was safest to follow my lead. I realized what he was doing and started over, walking through the river and getting my feet wet. Apollo happily followed and ended up being quite the water baby.*

Chapter 14:
Horses in the Human World

It is important to understand how to create a positive lifestyle for our horses in the domestic world. Although horses have been domesticated for many generations, the root of who they are is still tied to the wild horses that ran free over the land. So many of the behavior problems I see can be resolved by adapting the lifestyle of the horse. This does not mean that all horses have to live in big pastures and herds. In fact, for some horses that have lived in a stall their whole lives, this may seem overwhelming. It just means that by recognizing the instinctual needs that are getting met in a more natural lifestyle, we can find ways to create it within the show barn or domestic world in which our horses live.

Movement

In the wild, horses are moving all day long. They graze, they walk down to the water hole, they roll, and they get up for a buck. Each horse has an individual energy level, but all horses need movement. The energy level just defines how much movement and what type of movement. While riding and lunging a horse provides movement and exercise, it may not provide the type or amount that your horse needs. This is also controlled by us rather than allowing the horse time to express himself through movement. Turnout is an important piece of a horse's well-being. It allows the horse time to express himself and play.

Lunging can be a valuable tool, but it is sometimes misused as a replacement for turn out. While the horse is getting exercise, he may not be getting the movement needed to release pent-up energy. A horse may need a roll and a buck, yet we are sending him around and around in a circle. He is not getting his need met and therefore is likely still expressing it in one form or another. At the same time, the more regularly we lunge him, the fitter he gets. It starts a vicious cycle of increased fitness, increased energy, and then an increased need to release the energy.

Social Time

Horses are herd animals and very social animals. They meet their need for social connection through various physical forms. Some examples are mutual grooming, sharing grazing space, and playing together. To prevent injury, it is commonplace to separate horses and keep them in individual stalls and turnouts. When this happens, we are taking away an important piece of what horses are. There are many ways we can reintro-duce this piece without having to turn them out together. Riding and groundwork should not be the horses' only social interaction. Being able to touch another horse over a fence, going on rides with another horse, and spending quality time with a horse in a paddock, stall, or field are just a few ways we can meet some of our horse's social needs. Again, we need to find a way for each horse to express and get individual social needs met.

Environmental Interaction

Horses are curious animals that naturally interact with their environment. This means when left to their own devices, horses will explore and have learning and stimulation around that exploration. Setting some time aside to take a walk and allow your horse to stop and explore things is a great way to get this need met. Another fun game is introducing new items, such as balls and cones, into an area where she can be turned out to explore. You can spend time exploring with her and meet a social need at the same time.

Chapter 15: Horses as Individual and Emotional Beings

Each and every horse has a unique and individual personality. This means horses learn and process information in different ways, they interact with others in their own special way, they have unique likes and dislikes, and they have their own individual set of needs. One of the reasons I feel it is important to share my knowledge with others, rather than a specific training regime, is that having the flexibility to meet the individuality of each animal is essential to creating a truly harmonious relationship.

These are the areas I feel are important to consider in identifying a horse's unique personality:

Horse's Needs

Each horse is an individual being with his or her own specific set of needs. Personality type, breeds, age, sex, as well as a unique personality all influence a horse's needs. A few examples of needs in a horse are play, connection, mental stimulation, and physical contact. Learning what a horse's needs are is important in creating value in the horse/human relationship. A horse will always get his need met, whether in a positive or negative way. What this means is that a playful young gelding who needs physical contact and play will likely try biting, invading space, and even pushing us to anger if his needs are not being met in a positive way. By reprimanding the horse, often physically, the youngster is getting his needs met in a negative manner but nonetheless getting them met.

Another benefit of understanding a horse's needs is that it enables us to create a stimulating and rewarding training program. A horse's personality and needs will influence which disciplines he enjoys as well as what types of lessons he enjoys.

Personal Experiences

Horses are emotional beings who all experience life in different ways. Their life experiences make them who they are just as your life experiences make you who you are today. Two horses may have the same personality type with very similar needs but are very different in many ways. Perhaps one of them was raised on a ranch with very little human contact while the other was raised by a young girl who adored her. Perhaps one horse had all her needs met in a positive way by humans, so she is very trusting and affectionate while the other had all his needs met in a negative way and is therefore aggressive and insecure.

We do not need to know their complete history to interact with them. We do need to recognize that part of who they are is influenced by their experience. A horse that has experienced trauma may be very affectionate although she seems aloof and cautious. By being aware that an experience caused the horse trauma and caused her to be fearful, we can then work through that trauma and change the horse's mind/memory about the experience.

Energy Levels

The amount of energy that a horse possesses will vary depending on the animal. Like humans, some horses are higher energy and could even be described as hyper. These horses often need lots of turnout, possible lunging, and likely a regular work schedule. On the other end of the spectrum are the lower-energy horses that may even be called lazy. These horses often need less work, a stimulating program, and can often be left long periods of time without being worked. Of course, many horses will fall somewhere in between these two extremes.

Recognizing a horse's energy level will aid us in tailoring a program and routine that will enhance learning and create positive experiences. Simple ideas, such as making sure a higher-energy horse, like Bravo, gets regular turnouts and possibly a lunge or round pen session after a few days off, can make the time we spend with him more harmonious and fun.

Dominant or Submissive

While the degree to which horses express their dominant or submissive nature fluctuates in each animal, the fact that they have either a dominant or submissive personality does not change. Dominant horses like to be in control, to make choices about their lives, while submissive horses are happy to take direction and let someone else call the shots. Submissive horses will actually become more insecure when there is a void in leadership whereas dominant horses will confidently fill the role.

Understanding whether a horse is dominant or submissive will make training and everyday interactions easier. Dominant horses will appreciate feeling involved in the decisions and even thinking things are their ideas. Submissive horses will appreciate your confidence and see your assertiveness as a sign of good leadership. Once again, being dominant or submissive is only a portion of what creates your horse's unique personality.

Curious or Fearful

Horses can be classified as having either a curious or a fearful personality. Again, the level to which they express this aspect of their personalities will vary from horse to horse. Curious horses are very interactive with both people and their environment. They like to explore the world, are very active with their minds, and learn quickly. Curious horses will find ways to entertain themselves, even under saddle, if we don't find ways to keep them interested.

Fearful horses are very tuned into their instincts. They are quick to slip into flight mode and are sensitive to their surroundings. Fearful horses prefer consistency and repetition to help them gain confidence and allow them time to process information. When planning activities and rides with your horse, taking into consideration whether he or she is curious or fearful will help you create a session that is enjoyable for both of you.

Friendly or Reserved

Being friendly or reserved refers to how a horse interacts with other horses as well as with us. A friendly horse loves interacting with others and could be described as an extrovert. Any sort of attention is usually good attention for a friendly horse while a reserved horse usually only hangs around for something specific that she likes. A reserved horse often hangs back and enjoys her own space. She is an introvert. Knowing if your horse is friendly or reserved will help you decide his or her socials needs and the level of social interaction needed.

Conclusion

It is important to take the time to review all these areas when discovering your horse's unique personality. There are many variations within each area as well as many levels of the degree of expression that a horse may display. Remain flexible in your conclusions because it is easy to end up putting a horse in a "box" or having a preconceived notion of who you think he is or how you think he should act. Make sure to take into consideration all aspects of a situation. Many horses have been defined as high-energy horses when in fact their behavior is an example of the sympathetic nervous system being in overdrive. Treating them as high-energy horses only exacerbates the issue. Most importantly, listen to your horse, and he will share with you what is important to him.

A Lesson in Individuality

Apollo came to me at ten months old. He was a beautiful, laid-back, barely handled Clyde/ TB cross, and he was mine. I wanted a sensible horse that I could start from the very beginning, something that I had never done before. He was perfect. Being that we are drawn to horses that mirror ourselves, I ended up with a very strong-minded, often stubborn, yet loving horse that had many lessons to share with me.

I started Apollo as a three-year-old during my time studying Monty Roberts's methods at Flag is Up Farm. While Apollo was quite happy with the transition from me being on the ground to on his back, he was less certain about taking direction from me while I was up there. Coming from a hunter/jumper background with the knowledge that Apollo was a natural over fences, I was excited about our future in the jumping world. Apollo apparently had other ideas. When I asked him to turn left, he wanted to go right; when I asked him to go straight, he wanted to go left. I did my best to guess at what he wanted to do and then ask him to do it, but apparently he just wanted to do anything other than what I was asking. Going forward was not in his vocabulary; lazy would be a good description. Looking back, I can see how our relationship on the ground caused him to question my leadership, and over time things improved. He became more cooperative to the whole concept of being guided by a rider.

Over the next two years, I rode Apollo on and off, running into a few minor soundness problems along the way. When Apollo turned five, I decided to get more serious about his training. As

I started to increase his work load, he started to show signs of soundness issues again. I had shoes put on him, which helped, but I realized I needed to make a tough decision. Apollo was not going to hold up very well as a jumping horse. I loved this horse too much to get a few good years out of him as a jumper and in the process break down his body. I had to look at whether or not Apollo's physical abilities matched up with what I wanted to do. I realized what would be the best for both Apollo and me was to find him a loving home with someone who would find joy in the same things Apollo did.

I put the word out that Apollo was looking for a loving person to give him all that he deserved. By that Friday, I had two people lined up to come look at him on Saturday. Both wanted him as a western horse. Having never ridden him western, I decided I'd better give it a try before they arrived in the morning. I borrowed a western saddle from a friend and hopped on. He was unconcerned about the change in tack, so I thought it would be a good idea to teach him to neck rein and slow his trot down to a jog. Within ten minutes, I was riding him around in a jog turning him with the lightest of touches on his neck. I started to laugh; never before had Apollo been so willing to follow direction under saddle. Apollo taught me a huge lesson that day. Like me, Apollo had definite likes and dislikes, needs and desires. After all these years, I had discovered how Apollo enjoyed being ridden.

The next day Apollo found his new mom. He is a happy, sound, and healthy pleasure horse who is ridden western. Apollo and his new owner enjoy the same things and share a similar vision of what a horse/human relationship should be like. I am so thankful for the time I spent with Apollo. The lessons he taught me were huge, especially the one about listening to our horses and finding out what they enjoy doing.

Chapter 16:
It's About Partnership

Everywhere you turn in the horse industry, whether it is the traditional horse world or natural horsemanship, there is a focus on leadership and dominance. The line that separates true leadership from dominance has become blurry. With the rise of education around equine body language and horse psychology has come the misconception that any method utilizing body language and psychology is absent of force, aggression, and dominance. Many popular methods have introduced a less harsh form of dominance that is mistaken for leadership.

One of the reasons I am so passionate about sharing my work with others is the value that true partnerships add to the lives of both horses and humans. Over the years, my definition and understanding of leadership has evolved. Growing up on the show circuit, I thought leadership was dominance and involved aggression and control. In my early years as a horsewoman, studying horses and their trainers, I started to see that strong leadership led to a strong partnership. Horses live in our human world and respond well to an assertive leader who listens and looks out for their best interest. My understanding of leadership and partnership has continued to evolve, always leading me to a deeper level in my equine encounters.

Authentic Leadership

Today I understand that the qualities of a good leader go beyond the common characteristics normally associated with a lead mare. A great leader knows the strong points and weak points of every member of her herd or team. She knows how to support others in making use of their strong points for the greater good of the herd. She understands her own strengths and weaknesses. She knows that allowing a fellow herd member to step into his strengths can compensate for her weakness. She knows that her role as leader is to encourage the members of her herd to embrace their unique gifts and step into their natural power, and to educate them in being their own authority. A lead mare does not have the time to constantly tell the other herd members where to go and what to do. Instead she allows them to find their place within the herd and educates them when their actions step out of alignment with the herd's best interest.

When we slip into directing our horses' every move, making every decision for them, reaching for continuous control, and dictating how we think they should feel and react, we have stepped out of leadership and into dominance, even if we are doing these things because we love and care about them. When we are acting from a place of dominance, we are stifling our horses' ability to reach their full potential and, in turn, not allowing our relationship with them to deepen to the level we desire.

Leadership in the Horse/Human Herd

Your relationship with your horse can essentially be seen as a small herd of two. Within each herd, there is always a leader. In nature having leadership is essential to the survival of the herd. Therefore, if there is a void in leadership, another horse will fill it. This is also true of your horse/human herd of two. If at any time your horse senses a lapse in leadership, he will step forward and take the lead. Having a horse's trust and respect as his leader creates an enjoyable relationship with a willing equine partner. Knowing what is expected of the lead horse will aid you in creating true leadership within your herd.

To get a better idea of what makes a great leader, let's look at some of the qualities the lead mare in a herd usually possesses:

- Assertiveness
- Fairness
- Confidence

- The ability to make decisions for the good of the herd as a whole
- Great survival instincts

In a natural setting, the lead mare is the lead mare because she can make the best decisions for the survival of the herd, not because she is the most aggressive animal. She must make decisions that are in the best interest of the whole herd, and to do so she must be fair, confident, and assertive. In fact, if another herd member catches the lead mare off guard, she will actually relinquish her leadership position as her ability to look out for the survival of the herd has been obviously compromised.

To be a true leader to your horse, make decisions that will benefit both of you. Learn about the world from the horse's perspective and take it into consideration when working with her. Most importantly, listen to what your horse is telling you. A true leader creates wins for everyone involved.

By acknowledging your horse's thoughts and feelings, you will gain her trust and respect. You do not always have to act on what she tells you, but at least take the time to listen. Think of a time when you have been scared and told someone you were with. If he or she ignored you, you likely felt just as fearful if not more. If that person acknowledged your fear but remained confident, it probably lessened your fear even if nothing else about the situation changed.

A Lesson in Listening

My cousin Becky has a wonderful mare called Annie. One of their favorite activities is a ride on the beach. While Annie is happy to walk, trot, and canter along the sand, taking her into the water is a different story. On a recent visit, I went with Becky and Annie to the beach and experienced firsthand Annie's resistance when it came to the ocean. I rode Annie toward the water, and even though she understood the boundaries I set for her with my aids, she did whatever it took to avoid going into the water. By listening to Annie's responses to me and to the water, I realized she was scared. I got off so I could help her face her fear. As I stood beside her, I noticed her watching the break line of the wave as it moved toward her. I remembered how earlier she has spooked at the footing change in front of her. Annie was not scared of the water. She was scared of how it moved toward her. When I stepped out into the water and lowered my hand down to touch the water, Annie reached her nose down to watch and then touch it herself. Pretty soon Annie was walking cautiously beside me in the water, and then Becky was able to ride her around in it.

This is a great example of how listening to and acknowledging Annie's feelings allowed us to reach Becky's goal of riding her in the ocean. Sometimes acknowledging the horse's feelings may be as simple as noticing her friend leaving the ring and understanding why she raises her head up for a moment.

Dominance

Dominance is a part of creating leadership but should not be mistaken for leadership. As with humans, some horses are naturally more or less dominant than others. While dominance helps define a horse's rank within the herd, it takes more than dominance to be a leader. Understanding how to be dominant from a horse's perspective will help you establish yourself within the horse-human herd as well as aid you in creating leadership.

Horses establish dominance by controlling the speed and direction of another horse, as well as being in control of their own speed and direction. While aggression is often used in achieving this control over the other animal's movement, it is the control of the movement that essentially establishes the dominance, not the physical act of biting or kicking. It is more effective to be assertive rather than aggressive when influencing speed and direction. Assertiveness creates confidence and respect while aggressiveness creates fear and distrust.

The more drastic displays of creating leadership and/or dominance with horses, such as round pen work and hazing exercises, are the most recognized. In fact, the subtle control of speed and direction is most important in our day-to-day lives. Often the horse that pushes into his owner's space and intimidates the owner into moving out of his way is also difficult and more resistant to following direction under saddle.

A Lesson in Leadership and Dominance

Bravo is a great example of a dominant horse that challenged my leadership until I was able to direct his movement. While the simple act of directing his movement showed my dominance, it was my attention to his personality, opinions, and emotions that created my leadership. Although I took on the role of a dominant horse in the relationship, I made decisions that were in his best interest. I used my position of authority to set boundaries for him, within which he could freely express himself. I taught him what was expected of him in the horse/human relationship and what a human could offer him in return. My leadership actually enhanced his life as together we found positive ways to meet his needs, especially his need for relationship and social connection.

When Bravo found true leadership from both Leigh and me, he began to search for ways to please us and looked forward to his time with us. That is the difference between leadership and dominance. A horse that accepts your leadership will thrive, look to please, and become engaged in the relationship. A horse that is simply dominated, whether by traditional or natural horsemanship methods, will do only as much as he is asked and will likely become resentful or emotionally closed off.

Part 4: The Body Language of Horses

Me and my sister, Samantha, observing
a herd of horses.

Chapter 17:
The Body Language of Horses

An Introduction to Body Language

The body language of horses is a silent form of communication used by horses. Through body posture, positioning, distance, movement, expression of body parts, energy, and intent, horses use their bodies to converse with one another. The body language of horses is a primary source of communication between horses and is as vital to their communication as verbal language is to humans. It allows them to share their feelings as well as to give each other directions and ask questions.

Unlike humans learning and using verbal language, horses start understanding and speaking equine body language from birth. It is even thought by some to be an innate language that they are born knowing. In the wild, understanding this silent language is vital for survival because it not only allows the herd to communicate with each other regarding predators, but it allows them to do so without the predator hearing them.

The body language of horses is a universal language, meaning both domestic and wild horses speak it no matter what part of the world they are from. A horse from Germany could be moved to North America and be put in a pasture with unknown horses and immediately be able to communicate. A similar language is used by animals such as zebra, deer, cattle, alpacas, sheep, and many other herd animals.

The wonderful thing about the body language of horses is that although we are different in body shape and size from horses, we can communicate with them using their language. Horses are always watching and responding to our physical bodies. Whether we mean to or not, we speak equine body language every time we are with a horse. To a horse, the placing of our bodies, our posture, and how we move all communicate something. So if we are already using the body language of horses, we might as well take the time to learn it properly and use it to create a clearer understanding between our horses and ourselves. The best way to communicate clearly is to say what you mean and mean what you say.

Like learning any language, learning the body language of horses takes time and practice. Practice it until you are feeling and speaking it, and it no longer feels foreign. Horses are herd animals; it is their nature to share time and space with others. Spend time with your horse and let him be your teacher. Observing horses interacting with each other is another great way to learn the intricacies of the language as well as learning more about each horse's personality and role within the herd. Horses use their body language and body placement to control the movement of other horses and renegotiate their place in the herd. The horse that is able to control another's speed and direction is often the higher ranking of the two. The lead horse is able to control the speed and direction of the whole herd. By learning how to effectively control the speed and direction of a horse through body language, we have another tool to assist us in negotiating our leadership of the herd.

Listening to Horses

Understanding what a horse is telling you is as essential as being able to clearly communicate your message to her. Like humans, horses like to be heard. Sometimes just acknowledging that they are sharing is enough. A large portion of equine misbehavior is simply the animal wanting to be heard and raising her voice or body language until you hear her. As with children, sometimes a bad response from a person is better than no response.

As a herd leader, it is important to listen to what the horse is sharing and then decide the appropriate response. There is a fine balance between listening and responding exactly as she desires. Misbehavior can also be caused by spoiling a horse. Listen to your horse and find the correct time and place to let her have her time.

For example, a young horse who is very food driven may want to eat while being worked in an area where there is grass. Allowing this will likely cause an undesirable behavior to be reinforced. Keep work time as work time, but find a "free time" for the horse to eat grass after her work is finished and once she is untacked.

This example shows how you can take the horse's wants and needs into consideration and still establish clear boundaries and leadership. Understanding the horse's body language will help you achieve this.

Understanding Body Language

Horses are constantly sharing their thoughts, feelings, and emotions with us through their body language. If we are aware of the subtleties of this body language, even the slightest movement can tell us something, and we can detect what they are sharing from one second to the next. While each part of a horse's body tells us something, it is important to look at the whole horse to receive the whole message. Movement, tension, and placement are all things to take into consideration when we are listening to equine body language.

As with humans, each horse has his or her own style of communicating. Some horses are loud and boisterous with their body language, shouting out their feelings for the world to hear. Others are calm and quiet, whispering their message softly. However your horse chooses to communicate, the important thing is to listen and acknowledge what has been said.

Exercise 8: Observation

Learning to understand the body language of horses takes time and observation. Watching horses interact with each other is a great way to learn. When I was first learning body language, I spent a lot of time observing herds of horses communicating with each other. I watched how the dominant horses gave directions to the more passive ones, how the more passive horses showed their submission, and what the horses did when something startled them. Spend some time watching horses interact with each other. Look at all their body parts, observe how they move, and watch the path they take.

Chapter 18:
The Keys to Body Language

Energy and Horses

Body, mind, and spirit are all interdependent on each other and are all equally responsible for creating true harmony within ourselves and within our relationships with horses. Therefore, to create truly balanced partnerships with a horse, we must communicate through interspecies communication, horse psychology, and the body language of horses.

At the same time a horse is reading our physical bodies, he is reading our emotional bodies and intentions or our energy. If we are attempting to give a horse a message with our physical bodies but our thoughts and emotions are in conflict with that message, the horse will sense the imbalance. Our bodies will also give away our inner feelings.

Focus and attention are also important parts of body language. Horses are distractible in nature and are aware of their whole environment. Unless an outside stimulus creates a focus for him to bring his attention to and to respond to, a horse will remain in a passive and relaxed state. Bringing our focus and attention onto the horse will cause him to bring his focus and attention onto us and what we are asking.

Posture and Body Language

How you hold your body sends a message to the horse. Certain body postures will enhance your communication with horses. In general, assertive body language is used when driving or herding a horse. It is used at times when you are asserting your leadership by controlling speed and direction. Passive body language is generally used to invite or to ask a horse to join you. It can be used once you have established leadership to invite a horse back into your herd or when you are showing submission to a horse.

The reason I say "in general" is that there will be times when you are establishing leadership with assertive body language, and a sensitive or nervous horse will cause you to become more passive with your leadership. An example of this would be softening your body and your eye contact while still driving her forward, moving in direct lines and using confident movements.

There may also be times when you are inviting a horse to join you, but you need to take a more assertive role in your passive body language. For example, a more dominant horse may need you to walk quickly and confidently yet still soften your shoulders and walk in arcs and circles in order for her to follow you.

When you are learning the body language of horses, being assertive and passive are common phrases you will hear. Below are some examples of assertive and passive body language.

Assertive Body Language

- Standing tall
- Shoulders square
- Head up
- Eye contact
- Moving in direct lines
- Confident movements

Passive Body Language

- Rounded spine
- Rounded shoulders
- Head down
- No eye contact
- Moving in arcs and circles
- Soft body

Boundaries and the Zones of Responsiveness

Horses are surrounded by a series of zones of responsiveness and energetic boundaries that aid them and allow them time to make decisions regarding their survival. For each horse, the distance and area of these zones and boundaries will vary according to personality, environment, experiences, lifestyle, and the present moment. By becoming aware of these zones and boundaries, you can watch, learn, and even feel where they are for your horse. The zones of responsiveness will give you a better understanding of your horse's reactions as well as aiding you in communicating through body language.

As you approach a horse, the first zone you enter is the *awareness zone*. This is where the horse will become aware of your presence. He experiences the orienting response, searching for the disturbance that caused a change in his environment. This is a primitive response activated by the horse's reptilian brain. The orienting response may be as subtle as the eye moving in your direction or a flick of the ear or as obvious as the head and tail suddenly raising.

As you continue toward the horse, you enter the *decision zone*. In this zone, the horse decides what your presence is indicative of and reacts accordingly. If the horse senses danger, he flees; if he senses a friend, he may approach; or if he senses indifference, he may return to what he was doing. Within this decision zone, you can optimize your communication of the body language of horses.

The last zone you enter is the *into pressure zone*. Horses are into pressure animals and will instinctively move into pressure. For some horses, this pressure takes the form of physical contact while for others physical presence is perceived as pressure. Once you have entered the into pressure zone, a horse naturally moves toward you unless he has been trained otherwise. Using the body language of horses to create forward motion within the into pressure zone gives mixed signals to the horse and is a lot more work for the human.

Within each zone of responsiveness, there are energetic boundaries that you cross as you approach a horse. These boundaries may seem more subtle than the zones themselves, but if you stay present in your felt sense, they will greatly assist you in the dance of body language. The *Encarta* dictionary identifies a boundary as "the point which something ends or beyond which it becomes something else." Essentially, as you approach a horse and enter each new boundary, you are moving into shared space and into relationship with the horse. How you enter into this shared space will begin to define the parameters of your relationship.

Have you ever walked into a room and felt immediately drawn toward someone? Or have you ever been approaching someone you know well yet felt as if you were intruding? These are energetic boundaries that you are sensing. They change from person to person, from moment to moment, depending on how each person is feeling in each moment. You can notice these energetic boundaries with both horses and humans by watching their body language and, more importantly, by being aware of how your body feels as you approach. Staying in touch with your felt sense will help you understand whether it is most beneficial to the relationship for you to approach, retreat, or simply remain where you are.

The Driving and Blocking Zones

When communicating with horses through body language, where you place your body in relation to the horse's body is as important as what you are doing with your body. Knowing the correct place to be when you are "speaking" to a horse will enable you to be more subtle in your communications. This is true both when you are asking the horse to be with you and when you are directing her movement.

As with the zones of responsiveness, the driving and blocking zones may vary from horse to horse. The angles from which you communicate within each zone will also give your horse information on what you are asking. If you start with a basic understanding of where you want to be and then feel how your horse responds, you will be able to find the "sweet spot." This is a time to consider the magnetic or energetic connection between you and the horse.

If you were looking down at a horse from above and drew an imaginary line perpendicularly across the horse's withers, you would separate the driving zone from the blocking zone. The area in front of the line and in the head area is the blocking zone. The area behind the line and in the area of the hindquarters is the driving zone.

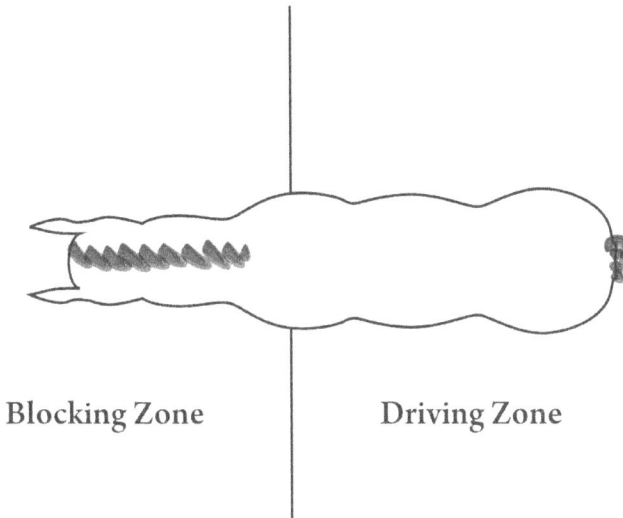

Blocking Zone   Driving Zone

The Driving and Blocking Zones

Below is a list of what you can communicate from each zone.

Blocking Zone

Assertive Posture—Driving, herding, lunging, etc.

- Change of direction
- Slowing down and even stopping of forward motion

Passive Posture

- Asking the horse to come to you
- Having the horse follow

Driving Zone

Assertive Posture—Driving, herding, lunging, etc.

- Creates forward motion
- Influences direction of forward motion

Chapter 19:
Body Language and the Round Pen

The round pen is a unique tool that allows us to create a scenario where leadership can more easily be established. My friend Emily Pelletier describes round penning as an opportunity to renegotiate a relationship. While there are many variations of round penning, most trainers/clinicians use body language to assert their leadership or dominance, depending on their training philosophy, in the round pen. *Join-up* or *hook-up* are terms used to define a conversation between horse and human whereby the human establishes leadership or dominance, depending on the process, the same way another horse would.

By controlling the speed and direction of the horse as well as sending him out of the herd, we can mimic the actions of the lead mare when she is schooling a herd member. At the same time, we are acknowledging aspects of the human/horse or predator/prey relationships and asking the horse to recognize us for who we are, not what we are.

An Overview of Round Penning

Following is a general overview of a round pen session. It is not to be taken as an all-inclusive description. A round pen session is a conversation between two beings. You can enter the meeting with an idea of what you want to discuss and your intended outcome, but how the conversation plays out will be dependent on the other party and how you communicate with him or her. Be flexible, and most importantly, when things appear not to be going as planned, listen to what the horse is telling you. An unexpected but necessary conversation may come up. This may then help you guide the negotiation back in the desired direction, or you may need to return to your intended conversation another day.

The first step upon entering the round pen with a horse is allowing him time to orientate himself. This means allowing him time to take in his surroundings and find out what directions of flight are available to him. This can be done by either turning him loose to explore or by creating a more controlled situation by showing him the directions—north, east, south, and west—of the round pen, in hand.

After the horse has time to orient himself, step back into the driving zone, usually at a forty-five degree angle from his head, and drive him forward around the round pen using assertive body posture. Sending him at the canter is the most common pace, but leadership can still be achieved at the trot and even at the walk. With sensitive horses that tend to be easily stimulated and overwhelmed, working them in the trot and walk is often more productive. *In the wild, the lead mare sends a horse out of the herd to teach him a lesson in appropriate behavior as well as to remind him of leadership. Being sent out of the herd makes the horse vulnerable to predators and reminds him of the value of the herd.*

Send the horse through his flight path, approximately one-quarter to three-eighths of a mile, in each direction. Direction can be changed by cutting across the round pen and into the horse's blocking zone. *By travelling his flight path in both directions, the horse has exercised his options of flight. In accepting a human as a leader, it is important that the horse is given the chance to follow his instincts and flee. This allows the horse to release any energy that may have been created in the perception of the human as a predator. It can also help release past trauma at the hands of a human which the horse has held onto in his body.*

After the horse has exercised his flight options, bring him to the direction in which he is most comfortable. If you are unsure, either is fine. Soften your assertive body language and allow the horse to bring his energy, pace, and activation level down. A trot is often most effective. The horse should start communicating with you as he would the lead mare. The inside ear will lock onto you, letting you know he is listening and willing to hear what you have to say. He will push his body toward you, often coming off the wall and bringing the circle closer to you. This is him communicating his desire to be with you.

As the conversation continues, be aware of the horse licking and chewing. This is sometimes recognized as a passive behavior, similar to the clacking a foal will demonstrate to an older horse, to show that he is a herbivore. As a horse processes information, letting go of old thought patterns and replacing them with new ones will cause them to lick and chew. Licking and chewing are also a way of releasing traumatic energy, which must be done to allow growth. Make sure you acknowledge this behavior by softening your energy and releasing pressure. This can be done through softening your body language and sliding your eyes away from the horse.

Licking and chewing is a very important piece of this conversation. It shows the horse is processing the new rules of the relationship and that he is releasing past thoughts and reactions. This does not mean that leadership issues or old behavior will never arise again, but that the horse is open to a new way of doing things and will follow your lead as long as he sees you being a true leader.

The last sign the horse will show you will be the lowering of the head and neck. The lowering of the neck and head is the horse showing you respect and becoming smaller in front of you, a sign of submission. By lowering the head and neck the horse is making himself vulnerable in your presence and sharing his trust in your leadership. *This is also a very important piece of this leadership conversation. By not only being submissive but also being vulnerable, the horse is telling you that he recognizes you as a true leader and is putting his survival in your hands. This is the horse recognizing you for you and not as a predator.*

Once the horse has shown you these signs and you have acknowledged his conversation, it is time to come together. By stepping forward into the blocking zone and becoming passive, you invite the horse to join you. It can be helpful to think of painting an imaginary line from the horse's tail to his nose with your index finger and following through with the motion until your hand is across your body.

Allow the horse time to respond. Some horses will come straight to you; others will need more encouragement. If the horse is looking at you but not moving, arc around him. The arc should be a rainbow shape from one of the horse's shoulders to the other and back, slowly bringing your arc closer to the horse. Any time that the horse moves toward you, stop your movement. If the horse stops before he reaches you, start your arcing again. *Horses naturally move in arcs and circles. They use arcing to invite and draw each other to them.*

Once the horse has taken the last step to you, reaching out to be with you, turn to face him in a passive manner. Take a moment to bond and give affection. Next, walk away from the horse in a figure-of-eight pattern, inviting him to follow you. This is confirmation of his choice to be with you. You want to be both passive and confident. *Enjoy this time. Your horse has accepted you for who you are and as a leader. You will hold this position unless he sees a reason to doubt your leadership. Trust and respect is a two-way street that is equally important to share as it is to receive*

When you are happy with the verification process, take some time to touch the horse's body. Carefully and smoothly run your hands all over his body, taking time to be aware of any reactions. Pick up the horse's feet; they are his flight mechanism. By giving them to you, he trusts you with his flight option. *This hands-on time is a great way to connect with the horse as well as to get a read on what his comfort level is.*

The most important thing to remember about this process is that every conversation you have will be different, even if it's with the same horse. Focus on what the end result is and recognize where you and the horse are throughout the process. Getting caught up in things going a certain way often makes it more impersonal.

Common Questions

The increased popularity of round penning in recent years has caused it, at times, to become simplified, shifting the focus from the connection and communication to certain specified actions and movements. When this happens, both the person and the horse lose out on the magic that round penning, and being with horses in general, can bring. Below are a few common questions I am asked about problems in the round pen and generalized answers that should help give insight into why the connection and communication are so important.

1. My horse always turns into me and wants to be with me but will not follow me. *It is common for horses to learn that when they turn in to us, the pressure is taken off, and if they do not turn in, they are being sent to work. Horses follow the path of least resistance, and learning the path of least resistance in the round pen is no exception. In many cases, the horse is turning in because she has learned the path of least resistance, not because you have established leadership. Therefore when you walk away she is not willing to follow and verify her trust and commitment to your leadership.*

2. My horse has given me all the signs but licking and chewing. *Many horses will*

IF YOUR HORSE COULD TALK

internalize their licking and chewing until all pressure on them has been released. When you become passive and invite them in, they will often then visually lick and chew. Licking and chewing is about processing and release. Some horses just need the pause that comes with the release of pressure to fully process and release.

3. I can send my horse around the round pen for an hour, but she still will not come all the way into me. *Highly sensitive horses, especially ones with trust issues, can easily get overstimulated in the round pen. When their sympathetic nervous system kicks in, they are no longer able to have a conversation and process information. Furthermore, if the flight response is overstimulated, they are going to stay in a place of fear and not want to be with you. When I work with horses that are very sensitive and easily stimulated, I actually focus my session on working at a slower pace and keeping the activation level of their nervous system down, sometimes not even asking for a canter until I have established a relationship with them. When I do invite horses with trust issues in, I focus on sensing and respecting their energetic boundaries. By showing them I understand and respect their boundaries, they more quickly gain*

confidence and trust in me. You can never force a horse to trust you.

As with any training method, round penning can be either extremely helpful or harmful depending on how it is done. The intention behind the session as well as the person's ability to stay present in the moment will affect the outcome of the session. At its best, round penning gives rise to a deeper, more meaningful connection between horse and human that often allows for healing in both the horse and the human. At its worst, round penning affords humans a tool to abuse, relentlessly dominate, and create a learned helplessness in horses.

Part 5: Training Horses

Monroe and I sharing a moment. Photo courtesy of Cheryl Burke

Chapter 20: Monroe

There are many horses that have touched my heart, but there are a few extra-special horses that have touched my soul. Monroe is one of those horses. I was initially called out for a behavior consult to help with some issues that her owner was having while leading this beautiful, golden, palomino mare. Little did I know the incredible journey that Monroe, her owner Cheryl, and I would share. Together we traveled through the anger and fear caused by Monroe's first experience with a trainer. I relied on my intuition and faith in myself and Monroe, as Cheryl and I walked with Monroe through fear, anger, trauma, and helplessness that often seemed endless. As we approached the other side of this dark tunnel, which symbolized the worst side of what humans do to horses (and ourselves), I experienced a whole new depth to what is possible between horses and humans. Once again I was in awe of the forgiveness and ability to heal that these animals possess.

The following are my beliefs about Monroe's experiences being started with her first trainer. I was not there and can only make conclusions based on my knowledge of the situation. The trainer was a natural horsemanship trainer, and I choose to believe she was doing the best she could in that situation at that time. Unfortunately, in both the traditional and natural horseman- ship industries, anger, aggression, violence, and domination are often the "default setting" when trainers are frustrated and at a loss of what to do. In our results-based society, the need for a fast, efficient outcome has seeped into both the show world and natural horsemanship world. An example of this is the "Trainers Challenge" event at horse expos, where top trainers compete over the weekend to see who is the most proficient in starting a colt. While I, at times, admire the skills that some of these trainers possess and are shar- ing with the public, I believe it can cause unreal- istic expectations and pressure within the industry.

Another issue I feel it is important to address is the fact that trainers are human. This comment may seem unnecessary, but all too often we are inspired by these talented individuals and place them on a pedestal, leaving them there to pro- tect the identity their egos have created. Growth and evolution are part of everyone's process, and often this means making mistakes and asking for help, even the revered trainers. By remembering a trainer is human, we can enjoy sharing our les- sons with them and remain open to egos being left at the gate.

The first few months of Monroe's initial training went well. She was smart and sensible, progressing quickly under saddle. All the qualities Cheryl had searched for in a young horse were present. Confident in the new skills Monroe possessed, Cheryl stopped being present every session and trusted the trainer to continue forward in the same manner. Unbeknownst to Cheryl or the trainer, Monroe was starting to suffer from selenium deficiency. Selenium deficiency can cause stiffness, pain, and cramping in the horse's muscles but often does not show up as an obvious lameness. In fact, Monroe was looked at by a vet who found no noticeable lameness.

As Monroe's discomfort increased, her attitude changed. She started to resist work and showed aggressive tendencies the more she was pushed. As a dominant mare, Monroe wasn't easily bullied into submission, especially when she was in pain. The aggressive behavior of both Monroe and the trainer escalated until one day when Cheryl was told she needed to become aggressive with Monroe or Monroe would hurt her. Deep down this felt wrong to Cheryl, and she made the decision to take Monroe home.

At home Monroe's selenium deficiency was diagnosed and treated. Cheryl gave her time off to get healthy. Although Monroe showed some remnants of the undesirable attitude, the degree of trauma caused wasn't apparent until more than a year later when Cheryl decided to start her back to work. Before she could even get her up to the work area, Monroe would explode into the air, bucking and kicking with all her might. This was when I received an e-mail from Cheryl. By our second session together, it was evident that just being led triggered Monroe's trauma, and she was unable to control herself. Furthermore, Monroe was not the only one who suffered from the aggressive and traumatic situation. Cheryl would freeze when Monroe exploded, leaving them both in a dangerous situation. Cheryl and I decided it would be best if I worked with Monroe for the time being, and using her other horses, I would also teach Cheryl the methods I use. Cheryl also decided to work through her trauma with my friend Deborah Marshall, a clinical counsellor and Advanced Epona instructor who specializes in Equine Facilitated Mental Health.

Monroe's healing path was lengthy and trying. I started out teaching her boundary work on the halter, so she could not only have choices but also so that I could have a tool to start working with the activation level of her nervous system. This proved challenging as just walking down the driveway overly stimulated her sympathetic nervous system, and when it was in overdrive, she had difficulty learning about the boundaries I was setting. With a huge amount of time, patience, and consistency, she started to learn the boundaries of the halter and line, and thus I could somewhat influence the activation level of her nervous system.

I started to introduce walking and halting on the lunge line and eventually included some trot work. On the lunge, another deeper level of her trauma surfaced. Whenever something stimulated her sympathetic nervous system, which at that time could be fear, anticipation, or excitement, she would explode into the air, bucking and kicking as if she was fighting for her life. It was not uncommon to hear her verbalize her anger at these times. After a spell of this, she would aggressively turn into me, often rearing up, high up over my head. During these intense traumatic releases, I would keep myself safe while standing my ground without engaging in a fight. Each release revealed more of her story as I began to understand her fear, anger, and helplessness. One of Monroe's biggest challenges throughout her healing process was learning she had choices. Her past experience had been pain if she worked and pain if she didn't; we can only imagine how miserable Monroe's life was at that time.

Each session was like a new chapter as the layers of trauma fell away. Even her anger had layers. First was the fight she gave for her life, over and over, as she still felt backed into a corner with no place to be safe. As she started to feel safe, her anger became her empowerment. She started to share her thoughts and opinions, but she yelled them, making sure she was heard. Again I stood my ground, listening to her but making my own decisions, never engaging in a fight. With time, Monroe began to see that she had choices and to feel empowered to make them and to understand that things could be accomplished without a battle. She had not yet found value in her time with me, but she had realized working with a human did not have to be a struggle.

Through times when many people would have given up on Monroe or accepted her present state as her true state, Cheryl and I persevered and held onto the glimpses of a loving and gentle Monroe. It paid off. Intuition is a large portion of my work, and alongside that is my belief that the horses will lead me to the correct lesson. My experiences with Monroe have deepened that understanding to include the possibility that circumstances will conspire alongside the horse and me if I am willing to remain present and allow the lesson to show itself. The biggest shifts came in Monroe when situations came up that mirrored situations from her past where she was unsupported by humans. With her newfound skills, she was able to react differently, and in turn I was able to show her a different way for a human to handle the situation. It was these sessions that led to her finding value in Cheryl and me and allowed the loving, sensitive being that she is to shine through.

Cheryl was present for every moment of my sessions with Monroe. She worked with Deborah on her own fear and trauma. We worked with her other horses to bring her confidence and skill to a level that allowed her to start working with Monroe. Her dedication to herself and her horses inspires me. Not only did she allow Monroe and me to work through things that were difficult and deep, she worked through her own fears and emotions and educated herself on a different way to be with horses. As a result, Cheryl has not only created a harmonious relationship with Monroe, but she has also created harmonious relationships with her other two mares, Kara and Oriah, as well.

Chapter 21:
The Role of a Trainer

There are many roles a trainer may hold in the equine industry. Some strictly specialize in training the horse, others specialize in educating the rider, and some work with both horse and rider. It is important to be clear on what you are looking for and what your trainer offers. Partnerships are created when two beings come together on common ground. It is important to clarify what you need to bring you and your horse closer together. Too much emphasis on solely the horse or solely the rider creates an imbalance in the relationship. It can also create an unnecessary dependence on a trainer or coach. The best kind of trainer will teach you and your horse to do things yourself rather than doing everything for you. On the flip side, never asking for professional help can be equally as damaging. If your focus is on improvement and growth, what you need from a trainer will become apparent.

Monroe and Cheryl are a great example of the success that can result from the growth and education of both horse and human. They are also a good example of recognizing when professional help is in order. Monroe's trauma was so deeply ingrained in her that having someone skilled and confident in working with traumatized horses was a must. At the same time, it made sense for Cheryl to work through her own fears. I work with many nervous clients, but in this situation, I felt working with Deborah Marshall as well as working on her horse skills with me would be the most beneficial for Cheryl. Cheryl's dedication to increasing her confidence and skills with her other horses paid off as it allowed her to start working with Monroe much sooner than if the focus had been exclusively on Monroe. It also allowed them to break through past patterns separately, so when they did start working together, the communications were clear and harmonious.

The following diagram shows how I define my role as a trainer. I believe it is my duty to teach both horse and human the skills necessary for their relationship and communications to become closer together and more harmonious.

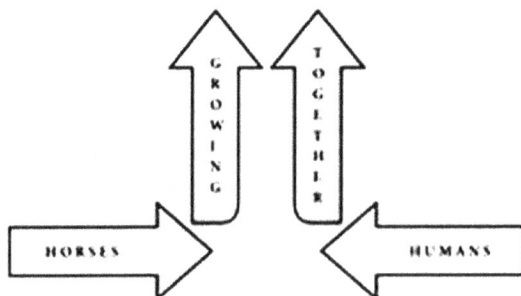

The Role of a Trainer

Chapter 22:
Creative Training Sessions

I hope that after reading this book, you will have a better understanding of your equine friends as well as many new concepts and tools to incorporate into your horse/human communications. Just as every interaction with your human counterparts varies day by day, so will your interactions with horses. Taking time to understand where you are, where your horse is, and what the goal is for the session will help guide you to what concepts and tools will be most useful.

I tend to keep my initial training sessions simple and spend time evaluating the learning styles and personality of the horse. It's important to discover what learning styles are more prominent in each horse as well as how well he retains the lessons and transfers what he has learned from session to session. Here are some areas to consider when working with a horse.

Creativity

Creativity is essential. There are numerous solutions to the same problem. If one thing is not working, try something else. Pinpoint what you are trying to achieve and search your toolbox for different ways to reach your goals. Don't be afraid to try something new or different. If everyone did what had always been done, there would be no computers or airplanes, and horses would still be our main source of transportation.

Goal Setting—Creating Intention

Setting goals for our horses and ourselves helps us gain clarity, focus, confidence, and a sense of achievement. Both long- and short-term goals play an important role in our success. Long-term goals create focus, motivation, inspiration, and the desire for growth. Short-term goals keep us on track, help us with the basics, ensure we cover all necessary steps, and give us confidence in our horses and ourselves.

It is important to consider all factors when you are setting goals. If your initial goal seems out of reach, focus on breaking it down into smaller steps. Look at what you need to do to achieve your goal, and remember going back to the basics is always helpful. And ask for help. Professionals are there to help you with skills, knowledge, and experience.

Here are some important factors to consider when setting goals.

Physical Ability—Horse and Human

Soundness, pain, conformation, size, strength, and endurance are all examples of factors that may affect a horse's or a human's capability of reaching a goal. Some limitations, such as endurance and strength, can be overcome by recognizing and improving them. Others, such as size and conformation, may cause you to permanently reassess your goals. For example, a fourteen-hand Arabian would not be a good choice for a six-foot-four-inch, 240-pound man to use as an endurance horse.

Mental and Emotional State—Horse and Human

One of the most important tools a good horse person utilizes is his or her mind. Check in with yourself and make sure you are emotionally ready to complete the task at hand. Some factors to consider are your mood, your confidence level, and your ability to remain neutral. Staying neutral and open is key. It is better to wait until you are in the right frame of mind and can create a positive session for both you and your horse.

Your horse's state of mind is also important. Take into consideration your horse's confidence level, attention span, focus, and mood when setting your goals.

Environment and Equipment

Having the correct environment and equipment is essential in achieving your goals. Do a safety check of the work environment and the equipment you will be using. Good footing, good fencing, and well-fitted tack can make all the difference in creating a successful session.

Choose equipment and an environment that is appropriate for both you and your horse. Set the horse up to win by using the environment and equipment to make the lesson as easy as possible. Footing, size of workspace, choice of tack, and activity in the surrounding area are examples of factors that affect the outcome of a session. For example, when I am getting on a youngster for the first time, I choose a time of day when the barn is quiet, and there is very little activity to help create a calm, focused environment. I make sure the footing is even and maintained so that the horse can adjust to the weight of a rider without being distracted by tripping or uneven footing. I use my own saddle, as long as it fits the horse, so I can be comfortable and relaxed. I have someone watching for safety reasons and make sure he or she knows to be quiet and calm during the session.

Skills and Knowledge

Education and the ability to execute skills need to be considered. It is important to be clear on how you are going to handle the session and to be confident in putting your plan into action. Learning is an ongoing process. Asking others for help as well as reading and watching other people work are great ways to increase your knowledge. Practice will increase your confidence as well as train your body to respond quickly and correctly.

Flexibility and Allowing the Lesson

It is important to have a plan and know where you are headed. This helps you set a clear intention for both you and your horse. It is equally as important to be flexible and work with your horse from where she is at. Flexibility creates more opportunity for harmony and growth. My success when dealing with a horse's undesirable behavior is largely due to my ability to stay in the present moment and allow the appropriate lesson to unfold. Rather than looking for a quick fix or surface solution, I focus on working with the root of a problem. A horse may bite for many reasons, and my goal is to deal with the underlying issue rather than handle all biters in the same manner. All too often the resulting behaviors, such as biting, kicking, rearing, and bucking, are treated as the core issue. When this happens, it is common for the behavior to resurface in another form or outlet because the true core of the problem has not been recognized and dealt with. Staying in the present moment and starting from the beginning allow the real issues and necessary lessons to show themselves.

As a general rule, I ask my new clients to leave their horses in the field, paddock, or stall for the first consultation. This allows me to see what happens from the moment the client approaches the horse. Frequently the client has just been noticing the extreme behaviors while the issues are actually apparent in the ordinary handling too. It can be much easier to start to work with these issues as they begin to materialize rather than waiting for them to intensify. Often this means working with the horse and client in an area that on the surface does not appear to relate to the reason I was contacted. When everyone involved focuses on staying in the present moment, an obvious and often simple path appears, leading toward the desired end result.

Having a general plan is important, but being willing to follow the flow of the lesson is even more important. Often circumstances will arise that completely change the direction of your plan. When you remain present in what is happening, a more important lesson tends to emerge. Monroe has been a great teacher on the synchronicity that occurs when I allow the lesson to present itself.

A Lesson in Allowing the Lesson to Unfold

Monroe had reached a point in her training where she was gaining confidence in her ability to make decisions and find the path of least resistance. She was interested in her sessions and had finally found some value in her time with Cheryl and me, but she had yet to let down and give us her full trust. Realizing that trust cannot be forced, I continued forward with her training and had faith the lesson would appear when she was ready. It did.

I arrived for our session with a plan to lunge her with the saddle on, something she had done numerous times. While my plan was relatively low key, I did notice a familiar sensation in my stomach, the one I felt when she had big releases in the past. I kept it in the back of my mind as I went to get her. As I was opening the gate, she came up to see me, and I accidentally knocked her nose with the gate chain. Her head shot up, and she smashed her forehead on the fence. She pulled back and stood pawing with her head down, obviously in pain. I went into the paddock and proceeded to softly touch her head, doing some Reiki and talking to her softly. Her body softened, she stopped pawing, and she began to lick and chew as she allowed me to take care of her. Cheryl and I both noticed an obvious shift in Monroe, and we discussed how she had many small accidents in her time with the last trainer. That was during the time when her attitude was strong, and we doubted highly that she had been given any compassion at the time.

Monroe soon perked up, and I decided to work her, feeling that the big lesson of the day may have already taken place. I lunged her with the tack on, and she was calm, focused, and relaxed. Pleased with her behavior, I decided to head back down the hill to the barn early. Cheryl walked ahead as Monroe and I started down the trail. After we were just a few feet down the hill, Monroe suddenly exploded, bucking and screaming as if the saddle was a predator. It was one of the most primal sounds I have experienced while working with horses. Standing back, I jerked on the halter and talked to her, doing my best to set a boundary that would keep both me and Monroe safe. A couple of times she paused for a second and then continued bucking and screaming. Finally she stopped with her back arched into the saddle and her body tense. I quietly approached her and started touching her. We stayed there until she started to relax. Slowly I led her down the hill, one or two steps at a time. I stopped her so frequently to regulate her activation level and to ensure she was in control of her body. She seemed fragile and scared as she allowed me to guide her down the trail.

Roughly halfway down the hill, Monroe started to cough dramatically, almost as if she was choking. Understanding this was somehow related to the trauma she was working through, I steadily reached my hand into her mouth checking for a blockage and rubbing her tongue when I realized nothing was there. I removed my hand from her mouth and stood quietly beside her. Her body relaxed, and she pushed her head softly into me and started gently licking me. We stood there for a time sharing this moment and then continued back to the barn. All Monroe's resistance seemed to fall away as for the first time she placed her trust in me and allowed me to safely guide her home.

From that day forward, Monroe has chosen to place her trust in Cheryl and me. Her dominant and intelligent nature still causes her to share her opinions at times, but her need to defend and distance herself from humans is gone. I still do not know what set her off at the top of the hill, but I do know never in my wildest imaginings could I have manufactured such a profound lesson or healing.

Chapter 23:
Essential Lessons for All Horses

Horses are incredibly willing and resilient animals. They have adjusted incredibly well to the human world; so well that we sometimes forget that their natural instincts tell them to respond exactly opposite to what will keep them safe in the human world. Therefore, not only do we need to understand what a horse's natural instincts are, we need to teach them how to keep themselves safe and happy in the human world. This chapter includes the lessons that are essential for any horse at any age.

Choices and Boundaries

Creating true leadership entails setting boundaries for your horse and allowing him to make choices. If you are always saying "you must" to him, you are creating a dictatorship, not a partnership. Let's imagine how it would feel to always be told "you must" and have no say in your own life. Some emotions likely to arise are distrust, fear, resentment, anger, powerlessness, confusion, insecurity, lack of self-confidence, and a low level of motivation.

Now let's imagine what it feels like to be given choices and to be allowed to make decisions. It is highly probable we would feel worthy, listened to, confident, secure, powerful, engaged, trustful, and willing to please. The portion of a horse's brain that deals with emotion is comparable to a human's. This means how we treat our horses affects how they feel and how they experience interactions with us. By allowing an insecure horse choice we help him gain confidence in himself, as well as in us. By allowing an aggressive horse choice, we allow him to feel in control and powerful, which is most often what he is trying to achieve through aggression. By allowing a fearful horse choice, we allow him to take control of his own life first and in the process grow to trust us. And by allowing all horses choices, we allow them to search for what they like and what they desire and therefore create motivated, willing horses.

Setting boundaries goes hand in hand with allowing your horse to make decisions. While you want to allow him to be an active member in the relationship, it is also your duty to set boundaries for him to work within. Now some of you may read the word *duty* and think I am being dramatic. Let's remember that we have brought horses into our human environment, one that they often do not innately understand. Horses are large animals, and it is in the best interest and safety of both horse and human that they understand how to function and perform in our world. Allowing a horse choice without setting boundaries creates the potential for developing a very large and spoiled animal who can throw large and dangerous tantrums. Therefore creating boundaries and allowing choice creates a harmonious and enjoyable experience for both horse and human.

A boundary is defined as a point where something ends or, beyond it, becomes something else. Personal boundaries are essential when working with horses. Recognizing the boundaries of what is your space and at what point it transforms to shared space with your horse is important for safety concerns as well as for establishing leadership. Horses naturally set boundaries, but unlike humans, they attach no stories and do not take them personally. A common misapprehension I come across when teaching clients to set personal boundaries is that the horse will be offended and no longer want to be with them. Horses do not take this clarification of boundaries personally. In fact, the relationship usually blossoms as the horse understands his place in relation to the human.

In Harmonious Horsemanship, I use boundaries to create a space or place wherein the horse can function freely, while experiencing comfort and the ability to be himself. Depending on what we are doing, the size of the boundary can change. Understanding and using the six directions of the horse are an important part of boundary setting.

Horses have six directions, forward, backward, right, left, up, and down. Kost Karazissis, a jumper trainer at Far West Farms, taught me a wonderful explanation regarding this.

Imagine your horse in a three-dimensional box. Now imagine you can remove any side of the box when you want. You can also close any side of the box any time you want. You can even push the sides of the box closer or farther away from your horse. Label each side of the box with the appropriate direction—right, left, forward, back, up, and down.

Horse in a Box

Box of Directions

Now take some time to play with the box and influence your horse's movement. Walking forward—open the front side. Does your horse walk out, or do you need to close or push in another side or sides to create the forward movement? Each horse is different. Backing up—open the back side. See if you need to adjust the other side or not to cause your horse to back up.

What happens when you close and push on front, back, right, and left and the up side is open? Often horses that buck, rear, or leap want forward motion, yet we are closing the front, sides, and back door. Horses most often try up before trying down.

In real life, the sides of this box are formed by pressure. Pressure can be present in the physical form such as your legs against a horse's side, your hands closing on the reins and pulling back on the bit, a whip, a wall in the arena, a halter, and many other ways. You can also apply pressure without physical touch. Through association, a horse can relate certain types of pressure to certain situations. A horse who is fearful of something may feel pressure from its presence even if it is present in a neutral form. Take a few moments to consider how this relates to your everyday experience with horses.

In setting boundaries for horses, we must create a box for them to function within and allow them to be free from pressure when they are in it. This box can move with them as they are ridden, lunged, led, or handled.

This leads to how we can allow our horses choices regarding these boundaries we are setting. It is the same choice we will give them in so many aspects of training—uncomfortable versus comfortable. Pressure is uncomfortable for a horse. The freedom from pressure is comfortable.

For example, when I am leading a horse, I will decide on the dimensions of the boundaries I am creating. I decide to create a box that allows the horse a foot of rope and a specific distance of space between him and me. When the horse walks, stops, turns, or jogs beside me while staying within these boundaries, I leave the line loose. There is no pressure on the horse. I am creating a comfortable place for him. If he makes the choice to leave the boundaries, he will reach the end of the amount of lead I gave him and hit pressure. The pressure will remain on until he returns within the boundaries. Horses are naturally into pressure animals, and it's important to make sure we teach them to move off of pressure before starting an exercise such as this.

Halter work is a great way to teach horses about boundaries and the choices they have in regards to these boundaries. Not only can I create boundaries through halter work, but I can also transfer them to new situations. Once a horse understands the boundaries created by a halter work session, I can take the session to a trailer. While the horse may not understand or like the trailer, he understands the boundaries set by the halter and therefore being applied to loading in the trailer. I can transfer the lesson to teaching a horse to walk through water, to lead into areas he is scared of, and even to start to introduce moving off of pressure to a horse that pulls back.

Taking the Box to the Saddle

The flat work program taught by Nick Karazissis at Far West Farms is a great example of his brother Kost's Box of Directions explanation put to use. The following is an example of how I used Nick's flat work program to prepare the many horses I rode at Far West.

I start out letting the horse walk around the ring for a few minutes on a long rein, allowing him to take in the surroundings before I ask for his full attention. This is something I do with every horse I ride as I feel this orientation time helps each one to relax and focus on me.

I pick up the reins and start with some walk/ halt transitions. This is practicing the opening and closing of the front door with some help or pressure on the side and back doors to push him through the open front door. I then add a few steps backward from the halt. This is adding in the use of the back door and using the front and side doors to encourage the horse backward.

I have now established the boundaries of the front and back door with the assistance of the side doors.

I move on to doing walking turn on the forehand and walking turn on the haunches to work on opening and closing the side doors. As I move the haunch or shoulder to the left, I open the left door with my left aids and apply pressure on the right door with my right aids to encourage movement to the left and vice versa. I have now set the boundaries of both the right and left doors.

I now move on to transition work through all the gaits in my half seat, the jumping position where the rider's weight is off the horse's back. By going up and down through the gaits, I am reinforcing the boundaries I have introduced. I am staying in the half seat, essentially opening the up door, as I start preparing my horse for the introduction of the up direction.

The next step is taking up a contact on the reins, getting back in the tack, and starting to ask my horse to come round. I have reinforced the basic boundaries and directions of the horse and am now ready to become more subtle and work on a less obvious direction, up. With an appropriate balance of pressure from front, back, right, and left, I can ask my horse to come up and round through his back. Soon I have a horse that is working within the boundaries I have set and searching for an answer to the next directions I give him.

You may have noticed that I have not focused on the down door in this exercise. This is because down is a direction rarely chosen by a horse in an interactive environment and in most cases is the last resort and a sign of resignation or giving up. The down door can be used in a positive way for such tricks as bowing and lying down.

Self-Regulation

By being aware of a horse's sympathetic nervous system and parasympathetic nervous system, we can actually work with her to increase the capacity of stimulation and stress she can endure while keeping her activation level balanced. In fact, we can actually teach her to self-regulate and bring herself back to a balanced state of arousal. A healthy nervous system is moving in flow between the sympathetic and parasympathetic nervous systems—attention and relaxation.

There is a ceiling to the amount of stimulation and distress an animal or human can handle before the sympathetic nervous system takes over. The majority of horses I work with on self-regulation are in a state of high activation and have to learn to calm themselves down. By working with a horse until she hits her ceiling or just exceeds it and then bringing the stimulation back down to a level that allows her to return to a more relaxed state and then repeating this, a horse's ceiling will slowly rise. She will also begin to learn how to bring her own level of arousal down, which activates the parasympathetic nervous system. As you teach her how to find comfort and safety, your horse will start to search for it as long as the stimulation isn't exceeding her ceiling.

Some horses respond to stimulation and stress by going into a freeze type response. For these horses, their responses actually slow down, and they often appear submissive. In this state, they may actually have both their sympathetic and parasympathetic nervous systems in high activation. This can be dangerous as these horses are frequently judged as calm, when in fact a great deal is going on. They have a tendency to react at unforeseen moments, often when the perceived danger backs away. When working on self-regulation with this type of horse, it is important to keep the activation level balanced, taking the pressure off but keeping the horse's attention.

When the sympathetic nervous system is stimulated, the following occurs:

- Increased rate of respiration
- Increased heart rate
- Increased blood pressure
- Increased sweating
- Digestion decreases

When the parasympathetic nervous system is activated, the following occurs:

- Slower, deeper respiration
- Decreased heart rate
- Decreased blood pressure
- Sweating decreases
- Digestion increases

Horse is over stimulated, unable to learn and often unable to control their body.

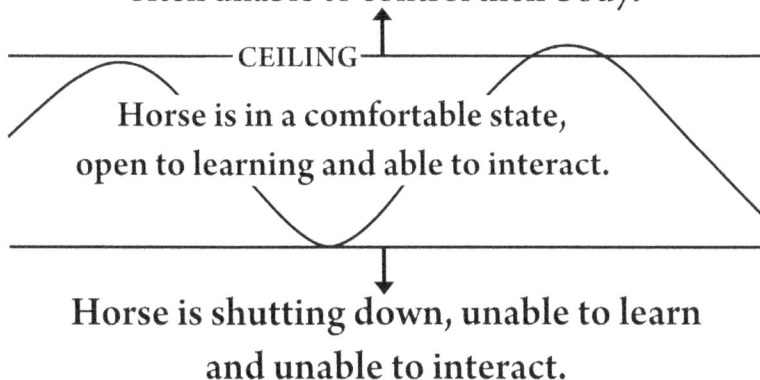

CEILING

Horse is in a comfortable state, open to learning and able to interact.

Horse is shutting down, unable to learn and unable to interact.

The Nervous System

Teaching Monroe self-regulation was important yet challenging. I quickly realized she was very sensitive to external stimulation and her sympathetic nervous system was activated very quickly. Her ability to control her body and think virtually disappeared when this happened, and she went into survival mode. Sadly, when she went into survival mode, she became more dangerous to herself as the trauma held in her body was triggered and searched for release.

I worked with Monroe to create boundaries on the ground as described on page 188. I used these boundaries to help Monroe stay focused and in control of her body while leading, and then transferred the lesson to lunging. Whenever the activation level in Monroe's nervous system rose, I brought her back to a lower gait, halting her if necessary, until she relaxed. Often I would go stand with her, allowing her as much time as she needed to return to a comfortable range of arousal. Over time, Monroe's reactions to stimuli lessened as did the activation levels in her nervous system. Furthermore, Monroe started to slow her body down and calm herself when she felt her sympathetic nervous system activating.

Essentially, self-regulation is the goal behind desensitization, although I feel self-regulation should be taught to all horses as they begin their working life. Working with the sympathetic and parasympathetic nervous systems of any animal should be done with the help of someone who can clearly understand where the horse is at and how to help her move forward. All too often desensitization goes wrong when the stimulation is applied and released at the wrong time or with too much intensity, and the horse ends up even more nervous and stressed than when she started.

When desensitization is taken to the extreme and the stimulation is applied to the point of the horse freezing, we often feel a false sense of security. When the horse comes out of the freeze and feels more secure, she will release the fight or flight response that has been stored in her body's memory. Even once this energy had been released, the horse will likely be no further ahead in her acceptance of the stimulation; sometimes she may have actually regressed. The only way around this would be to keep the horse in a perpetual state of fear once the freezing process has taken place. Not something I recommend.

Deborah Marshall, a clinical counsellor who specializes in equine facilitated psychotherapy and self-regulation therapy, gives a wonderful analogy of a container that is the range where a horse or human functions comfortably without overly stimulating the sympathetic nervous system. When working to increase the size of a horse's or human's container, the level of stimulation the nervous system can handle without becoming overly activated, it is essential that the facilitator's own container is larger. This is so that this person can remain in a calm state while guiding the horse or human client safely into an area where the sympathetic nervous system may be activated.

Of all the horses I have worked with, Monroe has been one of the most challenging for me to remain neutral, grounded, and calm with so I could help her move through the residual effects of trauma. When I first met Monroe, anytime she was stimulated in the slightest way, her sympathetic nervous system would trigger, her body going into fight-or-flight mode and her mind shutting down. As she experienced these extreme reactions, I had to create a container for her by remaining calm and grounded while directing her toward a safe place for her body. The halter work I did to create boundaries was very beneficial in this process. With guidance and time, the capacity of Monroe's nervous system has increased along with her ability to control her own body.

Another interesting note in the function of the sympathetic nervous system is the slowing and shutting down of the immune and digestive systems. This gives us a deeper understanding of why both horses and humans in highly stressful situations are often prone to stomach problems, ulcers, and colic.

Chapter 24:
Undesirable Behavior

Root of the Problem

Finding the root of the problem is an important part of understanding where your horse is. If you are working with an undesirable behavior that is the result of a physical issue, an emotional issue, or trauma, the behavior may disappear only to have another undesirable behavior pop up instead. Understanding your horse's individual personality as well as the psychology of the horse will help you discover why certain behaviors are happening. It is important to remember that the area of the brain that deals with emotion is a similar size in both horse and human. Horses are capable of strong emotion, and this is a factor to consider when looking at the root of a problem. If you are unsure about dealing with a problem, consulting a professional is always a great idea.

Monroe is a great example of the importance of recognizing the root of the problem. Had I just dealt with the physical behavior she expressed when I first met her, I would have only reinforced the trauma that she was experiencing.

Monroe's leaping and bucking were symptoms of the trauma she had experienced, caused by pain and human aggression. By recognizing that her behavior was merely a symptom, I was able to focus on what was really going on, a much deeper suffering. Monroe needed to heal and to learn once again to trust people. This meant actually avoiding conflict while still remaining assertive and helping Monroe remember what a positive relationship with humans was. Luckily for Monroe, she had already experienced this type of relationship with Cheryl. We just needed to help her experience it again.

As a trainer and as a horsewoman, I believe it is always my responsibility to ask questions when a horse begins to show behaviors that are out of character. If Monroe's previous trainer had done so, she would likely have realized that the changes she had made to Monroe's diet, in an area that lacks selenium in its soil, grass, and hay, had led to selenium deficiency. This selenium deficiency caused Monroe physical pain, which led to a change in her behavior and attitude. Sadly, the most common conclusion people jump to when a horse begins to misbehave is that she is challenging their authority. The first thing I like to rule out is physical well-being, which is then followed by emotional well-being and trauma. Had I jumped to the conclusion that dominance caused Monroe's challenging behavior, I would have only reinforced the negative behavior. By recognizing the trauma involved, I was able to help Monroe work through it and discover a horse that wanted to build a relationship with me, even if that meant allowing me to lead.

Horses are herd animals; they do not naturally seek out conflict. There is always a reason for undesirable behavior. Finding the reason behind the behavior and focusing on solving it will create long-term positive changes.

Reasons for Undesirable Behavior

Any behavior, whether it is desirable or undesirable, is present for a reason. Instinct, survival, conditioning, habituating, and learned response are examples of why both humans and horses behave a certain way. All behaviors serve a purpose and have an explanation. By understanding and identifying why a horse acts a certain way, we can then go about solving the problem from its source. This allows for growth as well as a long-term solution. Below are several reasons for undesirable behavior.

Pain: A significant number of horses that appear to have an attitude problem are in pain. The first thing to look at when dealing with a problem should always be the physical state of the horse. As well as obvious unsoundness, there may be ongoing, subtle issues. In addition to checking the hooves and legs, check for back problems, neck problems, ill-fitting tack, muscle soreness, dental issues, breathing issues, and anything else you can think of. A vet can often help identify and treat internal issues such as an ulcer or even a deficiency that is causing discomfort and pain. Monroe's experience with selenium deficiency is an example of how pain can lead to undesirable behavior.

Trauma: When the flight and fight responses are thwarted, the horse often moves into a freeze response. If the body does not discharge the frozen flight and fight energy, it will remain in the body searching for a way out. This often leads to undesirable behavior. If you think your horse is suffering from a trauma, it is best to get professional help.

Memory: Horses think in pictures and are associative thinkers. If a dramatic event has stuck in their minds, you will need to find a way to change the memories in their brains and bodies to positive ones. Memory also applies to pain. If a horse has lived with a certain pain for any period of time, his body has learned to function in a way that causes the least amount of pain. The body often needs to realize the pain is no longer present before it will change how it works.

Misunderstanding: Always take into consideration that your horse does not understand what you are asking. Is he trained to do what you are asking? Remember horses have to be taught how to lead, pick up their feet, and be ridden. There are many ways to do something and many ways to ask. Perhaps your horse was trained differently than you.

Miscommunication: Take the time to be clear in what you are asking. Horses communicate through body language and energy. It is common for humans to speak with their body language and energy without realizing they are doing so and without realizing what they are saying. Even as you learn about equine body language and energy, it is normal for you and your horse to make mistakes as you communicate with each other. Take into consideration that your horse thinks he is doing the right thing. Look at what you may be doing to cause confusion and find another way to ask. The only way to learn is to practice.

Leadership: All horses are unique, and they have good and bad days just like we do. It is the horse's nature to test your leadership. The lead mare in a herd is the one who makes the best decisions for the safety and survival of the herd. If there is a lack of leadership, your horse will take charge. If humans in the past have overlooked the above list, your horse may have lost faith in human leadership. Take the time and think like a lead mare. Calm, assertive, and confident leadership along with decision making that benefits both you and your horse will create a happy, willing partnership.

Acceptance versus Fear

Horses are prey animals that are very sensitive to intimidation and aggression. Humans, predators by nature, have often used this sensitivity to create the results they desire. "Make him more scared of you than he is of the … trailer, jump, water, etc." is a phrase many of us have heard when confronting a problem with a horse. While this has created a lot of success with some horses, for others nothing seems to work. For all horses, especially the ones that nothing appears to work with, working through the fear to a place of acceptance is the best solution.

The problem with the school of thought that asks you to make the horse more afraid of you than his present fear is this: The horse is never actually working through his fear of the trailer, jump, water, etc. The fear is reinforced as you use intimidation and aggression to create more fear. As the level of fear increases, so does the activation level in the sympathetic nervous system, and in turn his level of learning decreases. In his heightened state, he fails to realize he has accomplished the task you have asked of him and is still in survival mode, now fearing you as well. The problem usually arises again when he senses less aggression from the human or when his fear of the object is raised above his fear of the human.

Like humans, horses are capable of working through their fears and accepting objects and

situations that in the past appeared unaccept-
able. While working through fears may initially
take more time, the results are long term and
create trust and confidence between horse and
human. This trust and confidence will carry over
to the next situation where the horse's fear comes
into play. Being assertive is different from being
aggressive. A horse may need to be pushed to
face his fears but in a way where the door to
learning, choice, and acceptance is open.

A Lesson from Jolly Olly

Growing up, I was very fortunate to have a horse
named Olly. Olly was a seasoned show horse who
had a very successful career as a jumper. Riding
Olly was a new experience for me as he was a
spooky warmblood, very different from Shadow,
my courageous Thoroughbred. Even at sixteen
years old, Olly was still very certain that water
jumps ate horses. As I would round the corner to
a water jump, he would start back peddling and
do his best to avoid the jump at all costs. I had
been taught to growl, spur, and smack him, which
sometimes worked but other times did not. Even
when it did get him to the other side of the fence,
I was left with a nervous, disorganized horse and
guilty conscience. I remember feeling sure that
this was not how I wanted to deal with things, but
also confused because I hadn't been taught any
other way.

One winter Olly's old trainer came to give a clinic. I was excited to take Olly, and my dad made sure we had many spooky jumps, including a waterlike jump for the clinic. Olly and I warmed up over some plain fences, and then it was time to face our fears. By this time, I saw my inability to deal with his fear as a reflection of my abilities. I waited for the usual pep talk on being more aggressive and showing him who was boss. Imagine my surprise when the trainer asked me to counter canter down the rail and across the ring over the spooky fence. I had done very little counter cantering in my riding career as it was, and I was certain I would not be able to get him over the fence. I was very focused on holding the counter canter, keeping Olly balanced between my aids. I came around the corner to the jump, and although he tensed, he cantered right over. We tried a few more times with the same result. I was amazed. The counter canter forced me to keep Olly focused and between my aids. I realized that being aggressive was not the only answer.

This was not the end of my experiences with trying to intimidate a horse into doing what I wanted, but it planted the seed that there were other ways. Over the years, the seed flourished, and I began to search for better ways. Now, supporting horses in working through their fears is one of my specialties, and I have helped numerous horses work through their water jump issues.

Trauma

While most of us are familiar with the word *trauma*, it is often hard to define. This is because trauma is experiential and what causes trauma differs from person to person, from horse to horse. In most cases, trauma results from an experience where the sympathetic nervous system activates the fight-or-flight instinct, reacting to a situation that is perceived as life threatening. It ends up in a freeze response when high activation is combined with helplessness. The activation remains in the nervous system creating future challenges.

When facing overwhelming danger, all animals will respond with flight, fight, or freeze. Flight and fight are the two most common responses while freeze is saved for the times when there seem to be no options left. The deep freeze response functions in two ways. The first is the chance that if the predator thinks an animal is dead, it may drop its guard giving the prey a chance to escape. The second is that in the altered "freeze" state, the animal feels no pain.

In the wild when an animal comes out of the freeze response, it will shake, quiver, and twitch. Think of a mouse that seemed dead, yet when the cat finally left, the mouse woke up and appeared to run and twitch on the spot before he ran away. Think of a person coming out of shock/freeze and starting to shiver and shake uncontrollably. These are both examples of the body releasing any energy or trauma that got stuck in the body during the freeze response. It is nature's way of releasing this energy naturally in a way that is not harmful to the body.

Unfortunately we frequently are not aware of the body's need to release the energy, and we try to act as if nothing happened. We not only do this to ourselves, but we also ask it of our horses. In the wild, a horse will naturally work through the release of energy. Yet in domestication, we not only stifle the flight/fight response, but we then suppress the horse's ability to work through the trauma and release it from his system. This is damaging both to us and to our horses.

When a trauma is stored in the body, the body will unconsciously work to release the trauma. It will recreate the situation in different ways in an effort to fully play out the traumatic scenario. Regrettably, because we are unaware of the body's effort, we once again repress the necessary release and sometimes create even more trauma in the body. Think of a situation where you have recognized a horse has a fear, and despite your best effort to stop her from acting out, she continues to overreact and never seems to get over it. Until the horse is allowed a safe situation to release the energy, she will not truly "get over it." This should be worked on by a professional familiar with helping to heal traumatized horses.

A Lesson in Healing Trauma

Becky is a great example of how using fear to deal with fear can backfire and lead to trauma. I received a call about Becky after her owner had tried to load her in the trailer for the first time since she bought Becky more than a year earlier. "Tried" is the operative word. Becky had a cut on her lip from a chain, and many well-meaning people had been defeated in their quest to load her, even once she was sedated. The problem was not actually getting Becky in the trailer, but keeping her in if she sensed in any way that the door may be closed.

The majority of horses I am called to help with loading issues actually share Becky's fear of the trailer door closing. I find the root of the behavior is almost always linked with actually being in the trailer. The resistance to loading usually occurs after the horse's fear has been ignored and a negative experience has occurred. Becky's story may seem extreme, but the unfortunate truth is that a large number of people have been taught various ways to trick, pressure, or scare horses into the trailer. These methods may work the first few times, but if a horse is truly in a place of fear, she will quickly reinforce her negative relationship with the trailer. This is what happened with Becky.

When I first went to assess Becky I could see that she was very scared and reacting from a place of survival. I discussed her history with her owner. It turned out although she had been told Becky hauled well, the previous owner had insisted on dropping her off. She had arrived later than planned, and Becky had come out of the trailer appearing stressed and in a sweat. This information alongside the story Becky was telling me led me to believe she had been forced through intimidation into the trailer that day and then spent a fearful, lonely ride to her new home.

Over the next week, I worked with Becky, teaching her boundaries, giving her choices, and helping her learn to regulate her nervous system. When it was time to start closing the door, Becky and I turned to face the door as her owner slowly closed it and opened it inch by inch in response to Becky's activation level. Her "container" grew quickly until we were able to close the door for just a moment before opening it again. It was during the opening and closing of the door that Becky started her "release" of energy. Although she stood willingly in the trailer, she started to shake and move her legs around. I comforted and supported her as she released the trauma from her body. All the flight-and-fight instincts that had been frozen in her body for over a year finally made their way loose.

Due to the safe situation we created, Becky was able to release the energy in a calm manner that allowed her to fully play out the trauma. Becky's body had tried to play out the trauma the week before when she was reintroduced to the trailer, but she had been so stimulated and overwhelmed, she only managed to create more trauma. In a week, Becky was successfully loading and going for trailer rides with an equine companion. I always like to have a calm companion for young horses being introduced to the trailer and for horses that are fearful of the trailer until they gain their confidence.

You may notice this section on trauma is written to include both horses and humans. Over and over again I see both horses and humans that have been traumatized and who have never allowed healing and release to take place. If you think you or your horse may be affected by a past trauma or are interested in learning more, I highly recommend Peter A. Levine's *Waking the Tiger*. It is possible to heal and let the body release trauma as well as to learn ways to allow the energy to release at the time of origination.

Chapter 25:
Simple Concepts Make for Great Training

Over the years, there have been some valuable concepts that have served me well time after time. Every session I have with a horse and a person is completely customized. Whether I am helping create a solid foundation for a horse using the essential lessons in chapter 23 or helping resolve an undesirable behavior, I am always adapting it to fit the horse and person. The following concepts help allow me to create positive training sessions with deep learning for both horse and human.

Attention Span

As with young children, young horses and those that have not spent much time in a working environment often have a short attention span. In the wild, it is important for horses to be aware of the whole environment. Focusing in on a specific thing for any length of time would make them vulnerable to predators. As prey animals, this is hardwired into them. Therefore, as we introduce them into a working environment, it is important to understand their natural attention span. By working within their attention span and then slowly asking for a small amount more each session, we can increase their focus while gaining their trust and confidence. If we were to immediately ask for a time frame of focus that was noticeably larger than their natural attention span, we would not create success for them. We would likely have horses that stay in a more stressed and less focused state. Yet when we set them up to win and remember the point of the lesson is to teach them focus, we will quickly reach our goals.

Create Value

Creating value for your horse plays a vital role in generating a willing equine partner. Your horse's unique personality will influence what creates value for him. For some horses, the physical or mental stimulation of being worked will create value. For others, it may be the time spent grooming or juicy carrots when they get back from their ride. One of my client's horses loves hearing "good boy." Whenever he hears those words, he perks up and does his best to repeat what he did to earn them. There are times when a horse finds no value in humans. With these horses, it is especially important to find out what is important to them. If you can create value for them in working, often finding value in the person they are working with will follow.

A Lesson in Creating Value

Ariel was a five-year-old mare that came to me to be started. While she had been saddled and bridled before, she had never progressed further. She had made it this far in life with only two months spent in training. During her initial month of training, she had responded well until she badly injured her leg when she got caught up in the electric fence of her turnout. The injury took a long time to heal, and she did not start her training up again until the following year. From what I was told, she reacted very differently to this second month of training. She was tense and reactive, often getting herself and the trainer worked up. The training only lasted a month this time around. I have no doubt trauma caused her change in behavior.

When Ariel arrived, she was aloof and seemed to find very little worth in humans or what they could offer her. It was a challenge to start her as the training process required that she confront distressing issues that did not come up out in pasture. Her aloofness, dominance, and past experiences left little value for her in working. Grooming and petting did nothing for her, and I was left searching for a reason for her to find value in participating in the training sessions.

This was quite an obstacle as not only did she not see value in spending time with me, but the time she spent with me often triggered past trauma. Ariel had many layers to work through. I believe the initial trauma was caused when she got caught up in the fence. For the most part, she was a very sensible mare, yet she was easily triggered by objects touching her body, especially her legs. She reacted quickly, going into survival mode, taking flight out of pure instinct. To make matters worse, once she realized she was still attached to a lead rope or lunge line, she panicked even further.

I believe that Ariel's second month of training had actually intensified the trauma. Often when trauma is not recognized, regular training methods can actually do more harm than good. From what Ariel shared with me, my assumption is that the more she tried to run, the stronger the trainer attempted to control her, becoming more tense and restrictive with the line. Ariel and I had many things to work on, but first I needed to create value for her to do so.

I rarely use food in my training sessions, but I was at a loss. I did not want to create a resentful and unwilling animal. I started giving her a small piece of carrot when I went to catch her and after every portion of the session that pushed her into uncomfortable territory. Every day I would ask a little more from her before giving her a treat. The shifts were gradual and subtle, but I noticed her willingness to participate and interact with me grew. I then slowly decreased the treats until I had a horse that looked forward to seeing me and gave her work 100 percent effort. This not only made working with her more enjoyable, but it also allowed her to willingly work through her trauma and accept me on her back.

Creating a Pause

Creating time for your horse to process information and allow her to settle is a great asset when working with horses. It's very easy to get caught up in the daily hustle and bustle of life and not allow ourselves or anyone else time to pause. Pausing or taking a moment to breathe and bring your focus to the present moment can help you realign with your horse and your authentic self. It will also allow your horse to ground and refocus.

All too often, we skip from one lesson to the next without allowing time for the lesson to sink in and the joy of achievement to be felt. I create pauses throughout my training session, including after each small goal is reached and when I notice myself or the horse anticipating or struggling with the lesson.

Slowing Things Down

In today's results-oriented society, it is easy to get caught up in achieving goals and getting things done. Slowing down and remaining in the present moment actually moves you faster in the long run, especially with horses. All too often I come across horses with gaps in their basic training. These gaps regularly occur not because the horse never received the lesson, but because she missed out on the actual processing of the lesson, as her human rushed toward the end result. It's very common to see people ask horses to do an exercise at the trot or canter before they can do it correctly at the walk. Horses are like us; they learn to walk before they can run.

Slowing down also applies to the bigger picture. It can be so tempting to jump into the next exercise as soon as we feel the horse do the current one correctly. Resist the urge, and allow your horse to revel in her success. Slowing your lessons down allows you and your horse to get the most out of the process. The more you get out of the process the deeper and more subtle the learning will be.

Pressure and Creating Space

Pressure, and the release of it, is an integral part of training horses. It is very much a part of how we communicate and give direction to them. It is also commonly the cause of a communication breakdown between horse and human. Although horses are naturally into pressure animals, they are constantly seeking the release of pressure. This natural desire for horses to be free from pressure is what enables us to train them to move away from leg pressure, yield to the bit and halter, and many other things.

For both horses and humans, pressure can be applied in many forms, including physical, mental, emotional, and instinctual pressure. It is important to be aware of the many different ways we can apply pressure. All too often we are aware of pressure applied by physical touch but unaware of other types. Pressure can also be applied by physical presence or even a memory. An object in the general vicinity, such as a fence, person, or another horse, may stimulate an instinctual, emotional, or learned response.

While a moderate amount of pressure is often a good way to stimulate a desired response from a horse, too much can have the opposite effect. In nature, when a horse feels too much pressure, he will move and create space or freedom from this pressure. As with humans, a horse cannot process information clearly when he is under too much pressure. Therefore it is essential to his survival to find relief so he can make a suitable assessment of the situation. Thus, flight instinct is activated.

This need for space from the pressure could also be considered space to think. In nature, when an unknown object or being enters the horse's environment, it creates pressure, as it holds the possibility of being a threat to his survival.

Flight instinct will kick in, and the horse will move to a position of safety, creating space from the object. Once the horse feels this release of pressure, he will take the time to further assess the situation. Once he feels safe, he will often move closer for further assessment. It is common to see a horse appear to yo-yo back and forth between approaching the object, running from it, and reapproaching. In fact, the horse is usually moving closer to the object each time it approaches and creating less distance each time it leaves. Essentially the horse is exploring the pressure he feels, finding out what is actual pressure and what is perceived, all the while creating space for himself whenever he feels too much pressure of any type.

When a horse is with a human, his ability to find relief from pressure is greatly diminished, as is his option of flight. If there is too much pressure, the horse will go further and further into survival mode, losing his ability to think and process information. In this situation, it becomes the human's job to help the horse find enough release of pressure, or enough space, so that he can fully process the situation. This may mean removing a physical pressure or even moving the horse to a position where he feels safer. If we find ways to create space for our horses, we not only open the door for learning, but we also open the door to trust and communication.

Isabella: The Art of Creating Space, Creating a Pause, and Slowing Things Down

My young horse Isabella is a master at teaching the art of creating a pause, creating space, and slowing things down. Isabella is an almost three-year-old Selle Francais/Thoroughbred filly, who had almost no human handling during the first two years of her life. She is a highly sensitive horse who is still discovering the human world. She is still very tuned into her flight response and often reacts more like a wild horse than a domestic horse. Since my end goal is for Isabella to be my riding horse, I am taking the time to build our relationship and her understanding of the human world on a solid foundation.

So far, our time together has consisted mainly of me grooming her and taking her for walks around the property. It quickly became clear to me that for Isabella to feel comfortable, and therefore be able to learn, she needed more pauses than the average horse. She also needed to be allowed to take the time to process information slowly and quietly. In the beginning, when we went walking, we needed to stop every five or six steps for her to remain calm. If I tried to rush her or did not allow such frequent pauses, she became stressed and flighty. When I allowed and often created the pause, making sure to slow these everyday lessons down, her comfort level with the situation improved dramatically.

For example, the first time I took her for a walk over to the neighbor's round pen, she was tense, nervous, and snorting constantly. We stopped every few steps, paused until she relaxed a little, sometimes even backed up a step or two, and then walked forward a few more steps. When we got to the round pen, we repeated the process. After a few minutes, she began to relax and explore the sand and the sides of the round pen. By the time we went home, she was noticeably more relaxed. The next time we went over, she walked calmly all the way to the round pen, only stopping once when I asked her to. Once we were in the round pen, she took only a moment before she started exploring. A boarder at this farm even commented on how well she was behaving. By creating pauses, creating space, and slowing things down for her the first day, I allowed her to process that this was a safe situation and settle easily into work during the second session.

The reason creating a pause and slowing things down is so effective when working with horses, especially sensitive ones, is because this is what they naturally do on their own. Isabella experienced all the outside stimuli on our walks as pressure. By frequently asking her to stop or allowing her to stop on her own at times, I created the pause she would have naturally created on her own. When she was tense or unsure, I asked her to back up a step or two, creating space for her from the pressure caused by the environment. I slowed things down for her, giving her time to learn and process, by creating a way for her to pause and create space within our interactions.

Focus on What You Want

I always focus on what I want to achieve when I am working with a horse. This helps me stay on track and reminds me to teach the horse to behave in the desired fashion. It is easy to get caught up in knowing what we don't like; it can be harder remaining clear on what we do like.

Jack is a great example of how focusing on an undesirable behavior can draw our attention away from the desired behavior. Jack was a young horse I was called about regarding a bucking issue. When I went to see Jack, I quickly realized that his real issue was that he did not want to move forward from the leg. The bucking was a by-product. When we allow our attention to be pulled away from what we want, a horse can actually learn how to distract us from it. Jack had learned that bucking actually distracted his rider's attention from asking him forward off the leg. Jack's riders were getting pulled into a cycle of bucking and smacking with the crop but accomplishing very little forward motion.

My approach was to ignore the bucking, which luckily was not very athletic. I focused on creating forward motion. When Jack did buck,

I just kept asking him forward with my aids and only released them when he moved forward from them, regardless of his attempts to distract me. Within a few rides his behavior had dramatically improved. His regular rider was also able to ignore any bucking and focus on forward motion. Although he tested her the first couple of rides, the positive results prevailed and the bucking stopped.

When the bucking no longer distracted the rider's attention from having Jack move forward off the leg, the bucking no longer served a purpose and ended. I regularly use this approach in dealing with other issues such as biting and pawing. It is important to recognize the undesirable behavior is being used as a distraction before moving forward with the training.

Breaking Lessons into Small Goals

Breaking lessons up into small pieces is also a great way to ensure your horse is clear in his understanding of what you are asking. Look at what your goal is and then take it apart to see what components contribute to it. This is a great time to remember the instincts, senses, and learning styles of horses. Things that seem normal and simple to us may require an introductory lesson with your horse.

Joey was a two-year-old gelding that had been handled very little and had never had his feet trimmed or handled. His owner asked for my help to ensure a positive first experience having his hind feet trimmed. A horse's hooves are necessary for his survival. The hooves allow the horse to flee as well as to fight. His instincts tell him to do whatever it takes to keep control of his hooves, especially if something is grabbing at them. This includes kicking.

Joey was very protective of his hind legs. He'd made it this long never having anyone mess with them. His owner and I worked together over a number of sessions and then had the farrier continue the work with us. Here is a breakdown of the steps we took to teach Joey it was safe to have his hind legs and feet handled. This is focused on his hind legs as they were more challenging than the front.

- Starting by stroking him at his shoulder, I moved back toward his hind end, watching for him to relax. I worked with him until he could stay still and relaxed as I ran my hands over his hind end and down his upper leg.
- I then progressed to starting at his hip and running my hand all the way down his leg. If he tensed or lifted his leg, I would stay at that area until he relaxed and then move my hand back up for a moment. I would

then continue down his leg, a little further each time.

- Once I could comfortably run my hand down Joey's whole leg without him becoming tense or picking up his leg, I started lightly holding his lower leg in different places as he stood with it on the ground. If he kicked out, I relaxed my arm and allowed my hand to move with him. I did my best to only move my hand away once his leg was still. Joey's owner also started putting back boots on for him to wear in his paddock to get used to the feeling of something on his legs.

- After Joey was comfortable with me holding his leg as he stood, I started to lightly squeeze and say "foot." In the beginning, if he even lifted his heel off the ground, I would let go and reward him. Slowly I asked him to pick it up higher and would let go as soon as he picked it up. Again, if he did kick, I would relax my arm and try to stay with him until he stopped kicking. Joey was kicking to get me to let go of his leg. When I only released it when he stopped kicking, he soon learned that kicking did not free his leg, relaxing it did.

- The next step once Joey was lifting his legs nicely was to start holding them up. I started with just a few seconds and then progressed to more and more time. When he kicked, I followed.

- The holding of his legs progressed to adjusting how I was holding them and moving around to prepare him for the farrier.
- Finally, it was time for the farrier. Joey's farrier was patient and continued to handle and trim his feet in a positive way.

Conclusion

The noises around us drift off; soon they are a faint hum in the distance. Our breathing synchronizes as we enter the ring. The grass is short and springy under his hooves, absorbing our weight as we canter across it. The jumps are bright and colorful, vibrant reds and blues, contrasts of black and white. As we gallop to our first fence, the breeze rushes past our bodies, yet it seems as though everything else in the world has stopped. It is just horse and human united in harmony, in a common joy that comes from these moments together.

Our love of jumping, of performing, brings us together as we dance our way around the course. It is a give and take, as our synchronized bodies flow together. It is an intricate choreography of body and soul as we follow the pattern of lengthening and compressing, of winding turns, as the earth rises and falls beneath us.

This is my dream. This connection, this harmony with an animal, is what drew me to horses as a child. The idea that animals so large and so capable of overpowering us would let us on their backs, would willingly carry us, seems magical to me. Throughout my life, horses have continued to amaze me. Perhaps what I admire most about horses is their compassion and ability to forgive.

Horses have so much to offer us beyond ribbons and work. When I look at the relationships that are already being forged between horses and humans, I am inspired to explore where we can go from here. Every day I spend with horses, I learn more, grow more, and realize how much more there is to know. In hindsight, I realize when I have been most frustrated and unhappy around horses is when I have been most concentrated on the result rather than the process. At the same time, when I have learned the most and enjoyed the most, I was in the process with the horses.

Every result out there, whether it be the perfect hunter round, the perfect halt, or the flawless execution of a natural horsemanship game, became desirable for a reason. Along the way, people realized when the horse and human were in true harmony, in true connection, in true partnership, this is how the end result showed itself. What we must remember is that it was the process, the journey, which allowed the moment of perfection, of harmony, of connection. No amount of quick fixing, no perfect piece of equipment, no gifted trainer can replace the learning that being in the process will bring; although there are gifted trainers, helpful equipment, and many useful concepts and methods that will enhance your journey with your horse. Just remember to ask yourself, "Why horses?" and enjoy what it brings.

A minimum of 10% of the royalties from each book will be donated to non-profit organizations that either help horses in need or help humans with the help of horses.

To access our blog, free resources and the latest information and upcoming events please visit:

www.HarmoniousHorsemanship.com

www.ingramcontent.com/pod-product-compliance
Lightning Source LLC
Chambersburg PA
CBHW062209270326
41930CB00009B/1695